Test-Driven Machine Learning

Control your machine learning algorithms using test-driven development to achieve quantifiable milestones

Justin Bozonier

BIRMINGHAM - MUMBAI

Test-Driven Machine Learning

First published: November 2015

Production reference: 1231115

Published by Packt Publishing Ltd.
Livery Place
35 Livery Street
Birmingham B3 2PB, UK.

ISBN 978-1-78439-908-5

www.packtpub.com

Credits

Author
Justin Bozonier

Reviewers
Lars Marius Garshol

Alexey Grigorev

Commissioning Editor
Dipika Gaonkar

Acquisition Editors
Divya Poojari

Llewellyn Rozario

Content Development Editor
Nikhil Potdukhe

Technical Editors
Rupali R. Shrawane

Copy Editor
Yesha Gangani

Project Coordinator
Paushali Desai

Proofreader
Safis Editing

Indexer
Tejal Daruwale Soni

Graphics
Jason Monteiro

Production Coordinator
Melwyn Dsa

Cover Work
Melwyn Dsa

About the Author

Justin Bozonier is a data scientist living in Chicago. He is currently a Senior Data Scientist at GrubHub. He has led the development of their custom analytics platform and also led the development of their first real time split test analysis platform which utilized Bayesian Statistics. In addition he has developed machine learning models for data mining as well as for prototyping product enhancements. Justin's software development expertise has earned him acknowledgements in the books *Parallel Programming with Microsoft® .NET* as well as *Flow-Based Programming, Second Edition*. He has also taught a workshop at PyData titled Simplified Statistics through Simulation.

His previous work experience includes being an Actuarial Systems Developer at Milliman, Inc., contracting as a Software Development Engineer II at Microsoft, and working as a Sr. Data Analyst and Lead Developer at Cheezburger Network amongst other experience.

Savannah Bozonier — the best partner I've ever had in life. Time and again she has made room in her life so I can push myself to do things that take an immense amount of time. Things like writing this book.

My friends and colleagues for their support and help which culminated in this book: Tom Hayden, Drew Fustin, and Andrew Slotnick.

My mentors across the years — Chad Boyer, Kelly Leahy, Robert Ream, James Thigpen, and Loren Bast.

My parents — I don't know what it's like to be told I can't do something. My life reflects that in every way.

About the Reviewers

Lars Marius Garshol has worked as a consultant, product developer, and open source developer for two decades. He added Unicode support to the Opera web browser, edited a number of ISO standards, and developed the query language *tolog*. Later, he worked as an enterprise architect and an R&D developer. He is the developer of Duke, an open source tool for identifying near-duplicate database records. He wrote Definitive XML Application Development, published in 2002. Currently he is a software engineer at Schibsted Products & Technology in Oslo, Norway. He's working on a book on Norwegian farmhouse ale.

Alexey Grigorev is an experienced software developer and data scientist with five years of professional experience. In his day-to-day job, he actively uses R and Python for data cleaning, data analysis, and modeling. He believes that testing is not only an integral part of software development, but it is also very useful for building machine learning models.

www.PacktPub.com

Support files, eBooks, discount offers, and more

For support files and downloads related to your book, please visit www.PacktPub.com.

Did you know that Packt offers eBook versions of every book published, with PDF and ePub files available? You can upgrade to the eBook version at www.PacktPub.com and as a print book customer, you are entitled to a discount on the eBook copy. Get in touch with us at service@packtpub.com for more details.

At www.PacktPub.com, you can also read a collection of free technical articles, sign up for a range of free newsletters and receive exclusive discounts and offers on Packt books and eBooks.

https://www2.packtpub.com/books/subscription/packtlib

Do you need instant solutions to your IT questions? PacktLib is Packt's online digital book library. Here, you can search, access, and read Packt's entire library of books.

Why subscribe?

- Fully searchable across every book published by Packt
- Copy and paste, print, and bookmark content
- On demand and accessible via a web browser

Free access for Packt account holders

If you have an account with Packt at www.PacktPub.com, you can use this to access PacktLib today and view 9 entirely free books. Simply use your login credentials for immediate access.

Table of Contents

Preface

Consistent, steady improvement is the name of the game in Machine Learning. Sometimes you find yourself implementing an algorithm from scratch; sometimes you're pulling in libraries. You always need the option to try new algorithms and improve performance. Simultaneously, you need to know that performance doesn't degrade.

You could just ask an expert about every change because testing stochastic algorithms seems impossible. That's just as terribly slow as it sounds. What if you could automate checking that your updated algorithms outperform your previous ones? What if you could design your code so that you could swap in an algorithm from another library or pit one that you wrote yourself against what you have? These are all reasons for this book.

We'll be covering what test-driven development is and what value it brings to machine learning. We'll be using nosetests in Python 2.7 to develop our tests. For machine-learning algorithms, we will be using Statsmodels and sci-kit learn. Statsmodels has some great implementations of regression. sci-kit learn is useful for its plethora of supported classification algorithms.

What this book covers

Chapter 1, *Introducing to Test-Driven Machine Learning*, explains what Test-Driven Development is, what it looks like, and how it is done in practice.

Chapter 2, *Perceptively Testing a Perceptron*, develops a perceptron from scratch and defines its behavior even though it behaves non-deterministically.

Chapter 3, *Exploring the Unknown with Multi-armed Bandits*, introduces multi-armed bandit problems, testing different algorithms, and iterating on their performance.

Chapter 4, *Predicting Values with Regression*, uses statsmodels to implement regression and report on key performance metrics. We will also explore tuning the model.

Chapter 5, *Making Decisions Black and White with Logistic Regression*, continues exploring regression as well as quantifying quality of this different type of it. We will use statsmodels again to create our regression models.

Chapter 6, *You're So Naïve, Bayes*, helps us develop a Gaussian Naïve Bayes algorithm from scratch using test-driven development.

Chapter 7, *Optimizing by Choosing a New Algorithm*, continues the work from *Chapter 6*, *You're So Naïve, Bayes*, and attempts to improve upon it using a new algorithm: Random Forests.

Chapter 8, *Exploring scikit-learn Test First*, teaches how to teach oneself. You probably already have a lot of experience of this. This chapter will build upon this by teaching you to use the test framework to document sci-kit learn.

Chapter 9, *Bringing it all Together*, takes a business problem that requires a couple of different algorithms. Again, we will develop everything we need from scratch and mix our code with third party libraries, completely test-driven.

What you need for this book

We will be using Python 2.7 in this book along with nosetests to unit test our software. In addition, we will be using statsmodels as well as scikit-learn.

Who this book is for

This book is for machine learning professionals who want to be able to test the improvements to their algorithms in isolation and in an automated fashion. This book is for any data scientist who wants to get started in Test-Driven Development with minimal religion and maximum value. This book is not for someone who wants to learn state of the art Test-Driven Development. It is written with the idea that the majority of what can be learned from Test-Driven Development is remarkably simple. We will provide a relatively simple approach to it which the reader can choose to augment as they see fit.

Conventions

In this book, you will find a number of text styles that distinguish between different kinds of information. Here are some examples of these styles and an explanation of their meaning.

Code words in text, database table names, folder names, filenames, file extensions, pathnames, dummy URLs, user input, and Twitter handles are shown as follows: "Notice that in my test, I instantiate a `NumberGuesser` object."

A block of code is set as follows:

```
def given_no_information_when_asked_to_guess_test():
  number_guesser = NumberGuesser()
  result = number_guesser.guess()
  assert result is None, "Then it should provide no result."
```

When we wish to draw your attention to a particular part of a code block, the relevant lines or items are set in bold:

```
    for the_class, trained_observations in
self._classifications.items():
        if len(trained_observations) <= 1:

        return None
    probability_of_observation_given_class[the_class] =
self._probability_given_class(trained_observations, observation)
  [default]
```

 Warnings or important notes appear in a box like this.

 Tips and tricks appear like this.

Reader feedback

Feedback from our readers is always welcome. Let us know what you think about this book—what you liked or disliked. Reader feedback is important for us as it helps us develop titles that you will really get the most out of.

To send us general feedback, simply e-mail feedback@packtpub.com, and mention the book's title in the subject of your message.

If there is a topic that you have expertise in and you are interested in either writing or contributing to a book, see our author guide at www.packtpub.com/authors.

Customer support

Now that you are the proud owner of a Packt book, we have a number of things to help you to get the most from your purchase.

Downloading the example code

You can download the example code files from your account at http://www.packtpub.com for all the Packt Publishing books you have purchased. If you purchased this book elsewhere, you can visit http://www.packtpub.com/support and register to have the files e-mailed directly to you.

Downloading the color images of this book

We also provide you with a PDF file that has color images of the screenshots/diagrams used in this book. The color images will help you better understand the changes in the output. You can download this file from http://www.packtpub.com/sites/default/files/downloads/TestDrivenMachineLearning_ColorImages.pdf.

Errata

Although we have taken every care to ensure the accuracy of our content, mistakes do happen. If you find a mistake in one of our books—maybe a mistake in the text or the code—we would be grateful if you could report this to us. By doing so, you can save other readers from frustration and help us improve subsequent versions of this book. If you find any errata, please report them by visiting http://www.packtpub.com/submit-errata, selecting your book, clicking on the **Errata Submission Form** link, and entering the details of your errata. Once your errata are verified, your submission will be accepted and the errata will be uploaded to our website or added to any list of existing errata under the Errata section of that title.

To view the previously submitted errata, go to https://www.packtpub.com/books/content/support and enter the name of the book in the search field. The required information will appear under the **Errata** section.

Piracy

Piracy of copyrighted material on the Internet is an ongoing problem across all media. At Packt, we take the protection of our copyright and licenses very seriously. If you come across any illegal copies of our works in any form on the Internet, please provide us with the location address or website name immediately so that we can pursue a remedy.

Please contact us at copyright@packtpub.com with a link to the suspected pirated material.

We appreciate your help in protecting our authors and our ability to bring you valuable content.

Questions

If you have a problem with any aspect of this book, you can contact us at questions@packtpub.com, and we will do our best to address the problem.

1
Introducing Test-Driven Machine Learning

This book will show you how to develop complex software (sometimes rooted in randomness) in small, controlled steps . It will also instruct you in how to begin developing solutions to machine learning problems using **test-driven development** (from here, this will be written as **TDD**). Mastering TDD is not something this book will achieve. Instead, this book will help you begin your journey and expose you to guiding principles, which you can use to creatively solve challenges as you encounter them.

We will answer the following three questions in this chapter:

- What are TDD and **BDD (behavior-driven development)**?
- How do we apply these concepts to machine learning, and make inferences and predictions?
- How does this work in practice?

After gaining answers to these questions, we will be ready to move on to tackling real problems. This book is about applying these concepts to solve machine learning problems. This chapter contains the largest theoretical explanation that we will see in the book, with the remainder of the theory being described by example.

Due to the focus on application, you will learn much more than simply the theory of TDD and BDD. However, there are aspects of practices that this book will not touch on. To read more about the theory and ideas, search the Internet for articles written by the following:

- Kent Beck—The father of TDD
- Dan North—The father of BDD

- Martin Fowler—The father of refactoring. He has also created a large knowledge base on these topics
- James Shore—One of the authors of *The Art of Agile Development*, who has a deep theoretical understanding of TDD, and explains the practical value of it quite well

These concepts are incredibly simple and yet can take a lifetime to master. When applied to machine learning, we must find new ways to control and/or measure the random processes inherent in the algorithm. This will come up in this chapter as well as others. In the next section, we will develop a foundation for TDD and begin to explore its application.

Test-driven development

Kent Beck wrote in his seminal book on the topic that TDD consists of only two specific rules, which are as follows:

- Don't write a line of new code unless you first have a failing automated test
- Eliminate duplication

This, as he notes fairly quickly, leads us to a mantra, really *the* mantra of TDD: "Red, Green, Refactor."

If this is a bit abstract, let me restate that TDD is a software development process that enables a programmer to write code that specifies the intended behavior before writing any software to actually implement the behavior. The key value of TDD is that at each step of the way, you have working software as well as an itemized set of specifications.

TDD is a software development process that requires the following:

- The writing of code to detect the intended behavioral change.
- A rapid iteration cycle that produces working software after each iteration.
- Clear definitions of what a bug is. If a test is not failing but a bug is found, it is not a bug. It is a new feature.

Another point that Kent makes is that ultimately, this technique is meant to reduce fear in the development process. Each test is a checkpoint along the way to your goal. If you stray too far from the path and wind up in trouble, you can simply delete any tests that shouldn't apply, and then work your code back to a state where the rest of your tests pass. There's a lot of trial and error inherent in TDD, but the same applies to machine learning.

As a result, this whole process changes our minds. The software that you design using TDD will also be modular enough to be able to have different components swapped in and out of your pipeline. We will see more of this in the later chapters of this book.

You might be thinking that just thinking through test cases is equivalent to TDD. If you are like most people, what you write is different from what you might verbally say, and very different from what you think. By writing the intent of our code before we write our code, it applies a pressure to the software design that prevents you from writing "just in case" code. By this I mean the code that we write just because we aren't sure if there will be a problem. Using TDD, we think of a test case, prove that it isn't supported currently, and then fix it. If we can't think of a test case, we then don't add code.

TDD can and does operate at many different levels of the software under development. Tests can be written against functions and methods, entire classes, programs, web services, neural networks, random forests, and whole machine learning pipelines. At each level, the tests are written from the perspective of the prospective client. How does this relate to machine learning? Let's take a step back and reframe what I just said.

In the context of machine learning, tests can be written against functions, methods, classes, mathematical implementations, and all the machine learning algorithms. TDD can even be used to explore technique and methods in a very directed and focused manner, much like you might use a REPL (an interactive shell where you can try out snippets of code) or interactive Python (or IPython) sessions.

The TDD cycle

The TDD cycle consists of writing a small function in the code that attempts to do something that we haven't programmed yet. These small test methods will have three main sections: the first section is where we set up our objects or test data; the second section is where we invoke the code that we're testing; and the last section is where we validate that what happened is what we thought would happen. You will write all sorts of lazy code to get your tests to pass. If you are doing it right, then someone who is watching you should be appalled at your laziness and tiny steps. After the test goes green, you have an opportunity to refactor your code to your heart's content. In this context, "refactor" refers to changing how your code is written, but not changing how it behaves.

Let's examine more deeply the three steps of TDD: **Red**, **Green**, and **Refactor**.

Red

First, create a failing test. Of course, this implies that you know what failure looks like in order to write the test. At the highest level in machine learning, this might be a baseline test where baseline is a "better than random" test. It might even be "predicts random things", or even simpler "always predicts the same thing". Is this terrible? Perhaps, it is to some who are enamored with the elegance and artistic beauty of his/her code. Is it a good place to start though? Absolutely. A common issue that I have seen in machine learning is spending so much time up front, implementing The One True Algorithm that hardly anything ever gets done. Getting to outperform pure randomness, though, is a useful change that can start making your business money as soon as it's deployed.

Green

After you have established a failing test, you can start working to get it green. If you start with a very high-level test, you may find that it helps to conceptually break that test up into multiple failing tests that are lower-level concerns. I'll dive deeper into this later on in this chapter, but for now, just know that if you want to get your test passing as soon as possible, lie, cheat, and steal to get there. I promise that cheating actually makes your software's test suite that much stronger. Resist the urge to write the software in an ideal fashion. Just slap something together. You will be able to fix the issues in the next step.

Refactor

You got your test to pass through all manner of hackery. Now you get to refactor your code. Note that it is not to be interpreted loosely. Refactor specifically means to change your software without affecting its behavior. If you add the `if` clauses, or any other special handling, you are no longer refactoring. Next, you write the software without tests. One way you will know for sure that you are no longer refactoring is if you've broken previously passing tests. If this happens, we back up our changes until our tests pass again. It may not be obvious, but this isn't all that it takes for you to know that you haven't changed behavior. Read *Refactoring: Improving the Design of Existing Code, Martin Fowler* for you to understand how much you should really care for refactoring. In his illustration in this book, refactoring code becomes a set of forms and movements, not unlike karate katas.

This is a lot of general theory, but what does a test actually look like? How does this process flow in a real problem?

Behavior-driven development

BDD is the addition of business concerns to the technical concerns more typical of TDD. This came about as people became more experienced with TDD. They started noticing some patterns in the challenges that they were facing. One especially influential person, Dan North, proposed some specific language and structure to ease some of these issues. The following are some of the issues he noticed:

- People had a hard time understanding what they should test next.
- Deciding what to name a test could be difficult.
- How much to test in a single test always seemed arbitrary.

Now that we have some context, we can define what exactly BDD is. Simply put, it's about writing our tests in such a way that they will tell us the kind of behavior change they affect. A good litmus test might be asking oneself if the test you are writing would be worth explaining to a business stakeholder. How this solves the previous problem may not be completely obvious, but it may help to illustrate what this looks like in practice. It follows a structure of "Given, When, Then". Committing to this style completely can require specific frameworks or a lot of testing ceremony. As a result, I loosely follow this in my tests, as you will see soon. Here's a concrete example of a test description written in this style: "Given an empty dataset when the classifier is trained, it should throw an invalid operation exception".

This sentence probably seems like a small enough unit of work to tackle, but notice that it's also a piece of work that any business user who is familiar with the domain that you're working in, would understand and have an opinion on.

You can read more about Dan North's point of view in this article on his website at `http://dannorth.net/introducing-bdd/`.

The BDD adherents tend to use specialized tools to make the language and test result reports be as accessible to business stakeholders as possible. In my experience and from my discussions with others, this extra elegance is typically used so little that it doesn't seem worthwhile. The approach you will learn in this book will take a simplified first approach to make it as easy as possible for someone with zero background to get up to speed.

With this in mind, let's work through an example.

Our first test

Let's start with an example of what a test looks like in Python. We will be using nosetests throughout this book. The main reason for using this is that while it is a bit of a pain to install a library, this library in particular will make everything that we do much simpler. The default unit test solution in Python requires a heavier set up. On top of this, by using nose, we can always mix in tests that use the built-in solution when we find that we need the extra features.

First, install it like this:

```
pip install nose
```

If you have never used `pip` before then it is time for you to know that it is a very simple way to install new Python libraries.

Now, as a hello world style example, let's pretend that we're building a class that will guess a number using the previous guesses to inform it. This is the simplest example to get us writing some code. We will use the TDD cycle that we discussed previously, and write our first test in painstaking detail. After we get through our first test and have something concrete to discuss, we will talk about the anatomy of the test that we wrote.

First, we must write a failing test. The simplest failing test that I can think of is the following:

```
def given_no_information_when_asked_to_guess_test():
    number_guesser = NumberGuesser()
    result = number_guesser.guess()
    assert result is None, "Then it should provide no result."
```

The context for the assert is in the test name. Reading the test name and then the assert name should do a pretty good job of describing what is being tested. Notice that in my test, I instantiate a `NumberGuesser` object. You're not missing any steps, this class doesn't exist yet. This seems roughly like how I'd want to use it. So, it's a great place to start, since it doesn't exist, wouldn't you expect this test to fail? Let's test this hypothesis.

To run the test, first make sure your test file is saved so that it ends in `_tests.py`. From the directory with the previous code, just run the following:

```
nosetests
```

When I do this, I get the following result:

```
E
================================================================
ERROR: number_guesser_tests.given_no_information_when_asked_to_guess_t
est
----------------------------------------------------------------
Traceback (most recent call last):
  File "/Users/justin/Envs/default/lib/python2.7/site-packages/nose/ca
se.py", line 197, in runTest
    self.test(*self.arg)
  File "/Users/justin/Documents/Code/Machine-Learning-Test-by-Test/Cha
pter 1/number_guesser_tests.py", line 2, in given_no_information_when_
asked_to_guess_test
    number_guesser = NumberGuesser()
NameError: global name 'NumberGuesser' is not defined


----------------------------------------------------------------
Ran 1 test in 0.002s

FAILED (errors=1)
```

There's a lot going on here, but the most informative part is near the end. The message is saying that NumberGuesser does not exist yet, which is exactly what I expected since we haven't actually written the code yet. Throughout the book, we'll reduce the detail of the stack traces that we show. For now, we'll keep things detailed to make sure that we're on the same page. At this point, we're in the "red" state of the TDD cycle:

1. Next, create the following class in a file named NumberGuesser.py:

   ```
   class NumberGuesser:
       """Guesses numbers based on the history of your input"""
   ```

2. Import the new class at the top of my test file with a simple import NumberGuesser statement.

3. When I rerun nosetests, I get the following:

   ```
   TypeError: 'module' object is not callable
   ```

   Oh whoops! I guess that's not the right way to import the class. This is another very tiny step, but what is important is that we are making forward progress through constant communication with our tests. We are going through extreme detail because I can't stress this point enough. I will stop being as deliberate with this in the following chapter, bear with me for the time being.

4. Change the import statement to the following:

   ```
   from NumberGuesser import NumberGuesser
   ```

5. Rerun nosetests and you will see the following:

```
AttributeError: NumberGuesser instance has no attribute 'guess'
```

6. The error message has changed, and is leading to the next thing that needs to be changed. From here, we just implement what we think we need for the test to pass:

```
class NumberGuesser:
  """Guesses numbers based on the history of your input"""
  def guess(self):
    return None
```

7. On rerunning the nosetests, we'll get the following result:

```
.
----------------------------------------------------------------------
Ran 1 test in 0.002s

OK
```

That's it! Our first successful test! Some of these steps seem so tiny so as to not be worthwhile. Indeed, overtime, you may decide that you prefer to work on a different level of detail. For the sake of argument, we'll be keeping our steps pretty small, if only to illustrate just how much TDD keeps us on track and guides us on what to do next. We all know how to write the code in very large, uncontrolled steps. Learning to code surgically requires intentional practice, and is worth doing explicitly. Let's take a step back and look at what this first round of testing took.

The anatomy of a test

Starting from a higher level, notice how I had a dialog with Python. I just wrote the test and Python complained that the class that I was testing didn't exist. Next, I created the class, but then Python complained that I didn't import it correctly. So, then I imported it correctly, and Python complained that my "guess" method didn't exist. In response, I implemented the way that my test expected, and Python stopped complaining.

This is the spirit of TDD. There is a conversation between yourself and your system. You can work in steps as little or as large as you're comfortable with. What I did previously could've been entirely skipped over, though the Python class could have been written and imported correctly the first time. The longer you go without "talking" to the system, the more likely you are to stray from the path of getting things working as simply as possible.

Let's zoom in a little deeper and dissect this simple test to see what makes it tick. Here is the same test, but I've commented it, and broken it into sections that you will see recurring in every test that you write:

```
def given_no_information_when_asked_to_guess_test():
  # given
  number_guesser = NumberGuesser()
  # when
  guessed_number = number_guesser.guess()
  # then
  assert guessed_number is None, 'there should be no guess.'
```

Given

This section sets up the context for the test. In the previous test, you saw that I didn't provide any prior information to the object. In many of our machine learning tests, this will be the most complex portion of our test. We will be importing certain sets of data, sometimes making a few specific issues in the data and testing our software to handle the details that we would expect. When you think about this section of your tests, try to frame it as "Given this scenario...". In our test, we might say "Given no prior information for NumberGuesser...".

When

This should be one of the simplest aspects of our test. Once you've set up the context, there should be a simple action that triggers the behavior that you want to test. When you think about this section of your tests, try to frame it as "When this happens...". In our test we might say "When NumberGuesser guesses a number...".

Then

This section of our test will check on the state of our variables and any returned results, if applicable. Again, this section should also be fairly straightforward, as there should be only a single action that causes a change to your object under the test. The reason for this is that if it takes two actions to form a test, then it is very likely that we will just want to combine the two into a single action that we can describe in terms that are meaningful in our domain. A key example may be loading the training data from a file and training a classifier. If we find ourselves doing this a lot, then why not just create a method that loads data from a file for us?

As we progress through this book, you will find examples where we'll have the helper functions help us determine whether our results have changed in certain ways. Typically, we should view these helper functions as code smells. Remember that our tests are the first applications of our software. Anything that we have to build in addition to our code, to understand the results, is something that we should probably (there are exceptions to every rule) just include in the code we are testing.

"Given, When, Then" is not a strong requirement of TDD, because our previous definition of TDD only consisted of two things (all that the code requires is a failing test first and to eliminate duplication). We will still follow this convention in this book because:

- Following some conventions throughout the book will make it much more readable.

- It is the culmination of the thoughts of many people who were beginning to see patterns in how they were using TDD. This is a technique that has changed how I approach testing, so I use it here.

It's a small thing to be passionate about and if it doesn't speak to you, just translate this back into "Arrange, Act, Assert" in your head. At the very least, consider it as well as why these specific, very deliberate words are used.

TDD applied to machine learning

At this point, you maybe wondering how TDD will be used in machine learning, and whether we use it on regression or classification problems. In every machine learning algorithm there exists a way to quantify the quality of what you're doing. In the linear regression it's your adjusted $R2$ value; in classification problems it's an ROC curve (and the area beneath it) or a confusion matrix, and more. All of these are testable quantities. Of course, none of these quantities have a built-in way of saying that the algorithm is good enough.

We can get around this by starting our work on every problem by first building up a completely naïve and ignorant algorithm. The scores that we get for this will basically represent a plain, old, and random chance. Once we have built an algorithm that can beat our random chance scores, we just start iterating, attempting to beat the next highest score that we achieve. Benchmarking algorithms is an entire field in its own right that can be delved into more deeply.

In this book, we will implement a naïve algorithm to get a random chance score, and we will build up a small test suite that we can then use to pit this model against another. This will allow us to have a conversation with our machine learning models in the same manner as we had with Python earlier.

For a professional machine learning developer, it's quite likely that the ideal metric to test is a profitability model that compares risk (monetary exposure) to expected value (profit). This can help us keep a balanced view of how much error and what kind of error we can tolerate. In machine learning, we will never have a perfect model, and we can search for the rest of our lives for "the best" model. By finding a way to work your financial assumptions into the model, we will improve our ability to decide between the competing models. We will definitely touch on this topic throughout the book, so it's good to keep it in mind.

Dealing with randomness

Dealing with randomness in algorithms can be a huge mental block for some people when they try to understand how they might use TDD. TDD is so deterministic, intentional, and controlled that your initial gut reaction to introducing a random process may be to think that it makes TDD impossible. This is a place where TDD actually shines though. Here's how.

Let's pick up where we left off on the simplistic `NumberGuesser` from earlier. We're going to add a requirement so that it will randomly choose numbers that the user has guessed, but will also weigh for what is most likely.

To get there, I first have the `NumberGuesser` guess whatever the previous number was revealed to be every time I ask for a guess. The test for this looks like the following:

```python
def given_one_datapoint_when_asked_to_guess_test():
    #given
    number_guesser = NumberGuesser()
    previously_chosen_number = 5
    number_guesser.number_was(previously_chosen_number)
    #when
    guessed_number = number_guesser.guess()
    #then
    assert type(guessed_number) is int, 'the answer should be a number'
    assert guessed_number == previously_chosen_number, 'the answer
should be the previously chosen number.'
```

It's a simple test that ultimately just requires us to set a variable value in our class. The behavior of predicting on the basis of the last previous input can be valuable. It's the simplest prediction that we can start with.

If you run your tests here, you will see them fail. This is what my code looks like after getting this to pass:

```
class NumberGuesser:
  """Guesses numbers based on the history of your input"""
  def __init__(self):
    self._guessed_numbers = None
  def number_was(self, guessed_number):
    self._guessed_number = guessed_number
  def guess(self):
    return self._guessed_number
```

Upon making this test pass, we can review it for any refactoring opportunities. It's still pretty simple, so let's keep going. Next, I will have `NumberGuesser` randomly choose from all of the numbers that were previously guessed, instead of just the last previous guess. I will start with making sure that the guessed number is the one that I've seen before:

```
def given_two_datapoints_when_asked_to_guess_test():
  #given
  number_guesser = NumberGuesser()
  previously_chosen_numbers = [1,2,5]
  number_guesser.numbers_were(previously_chosen_numbers)
  #when
  guessed_number = number_guesser.guess()
  #then
  assert guessed_number in previously_chosen_numbers, 'the guess
should be one of the previously chosen numbers'
```

Running this test now will cause a new failure. While thinking about the laziest way of getting this test to work, I realized that I can cheat big time. All I need to do is create my new method, and take the first element in the list:

```
class NumberGuesser:
  """Guesses numbers based on the history of your input"""
  def __init__(self):
    self._guessed_numbers = None
  def numbers_were(self, guessed_numbers):
    self._guessed_number = guessed_numbers[0]
  def number_was(self, guessed_number):
    self._guessed_number = guessed_number
  def guess(self):
    return self._guessed_number
```

For our purposes, laziness is king. Laziness guards us from the over-engineered solutions, and forces our test suite to become more robust. It does this by making our problem-solving faster, and spurring an uncomfortable feeling that will prompt us to test more edge cases.

So, now I want to assert that I don't always choose the same number. I don't want to force it to always choose a different number, but there should be some mixture. To test this, I will refactor my test, and add a new assertion, as follows:

```
def given_multiple_datapoints_when_asked_to_guess_many_times_test():
  #given
  number_guesser = NumberGuesser()
  previously_chosen_numbers = [1,2,5]
  number_guesser.numbers_were(previously_chosen_numbers)
  #when
  guessed_numbers = [number_guesser.guess() for i in range(0,100)]
  #then
  for guessed_number in guessed_numbers:
    assert guessed_number in previously_chosen_numbers, 'every
guess should be one of the previously chosen numbers'
    assert len(set(guessed_numbers)) > 1, "It shouldn't always guess
the same number."
```

I get the test failure message `It shouldn't always guess the same number`, which is perfect. This test also causes others to fail, so I will work out the simplest thing that I can do to make everything green again, and I will end up here:

```
import random
class NumberGuesser:
  """Guesses numbers based on the history of your input"""
  def __init__(self):
    self._guessed_numbers = None
  def numbers_were(self, guessed_numbers):
    self._guessed_numbers = guessed_numbers
  def number_was(self, guessed_number):
    self._guessed_numbers = [guessed_number]
  def guess(self):
    if self._guessed_numbers == None:
      return None
    return random.choice(self._guessed_numbers)
```

There are probably many ways that one could get this test to pass. We've solved it this way because it's first to my mind, and feels like it's leading us in a good direction. What refactoring do we want to do here? Each method is a single line except the `guess` method. The `guess` method is still pretty simple, so let's keep going.

Now, I notice that if I've just used `number_was` to enter the observations of the previous numbers, it will only ever guess the previous number, which is bad. So, I need another test to catch this. Let's write the new test (this should be our fourth):

```
def given_a_starting_set_of_observations_followed_by_a_one_off_
observation_test():
    #given
  number_guesser = NumberGuesser()
  previously_chosen_numbers = [1,2,5]
  number_guesser.numbers_were(previously_chosen_numbers)
  one_off_observation = 0
  number_guesser.number_was(one_off_observation)
  #when
  guessed_numbers = [number_guesser.guess() for i in range(0,100)]
  #then
  for guessed_number in guessed_numbers:
    assert guessed_number in previously_chosen_numbers + [one_off_
observation], 'every guess should be one of the previously chosen
numbers'
    assert len(set(guessed_numbers)) > 1, "It shouldn't always guess the
same number."
```

This fails on the last assertion, which is perfect. I will make the test pass using the following code:

```
import random
class NumberGuesser:
  """Guesses numbers based on the history of your input"""
  def __init__(self):
    self._guessed_numbers = []
  def numbers_were(self, guessed_numbers):
    self._guessed_numbers = guessed_numbers
  def number_was(self, guessed_number):
    self._guessed_numbers.append(guessed_number)
  def guess(self):
    if self._guessed_numbers == []:
      return None
    return random.choice(self._guessed_numbers)
```

Downloading the example code

You can download the example code files from your account at http://www.packtpub.com for all the Packt Publishing books you have purchased. If you purchased this book elsewhere, you can visit http://www.packtpub.com/support and register to have the files e-mailed directly to you.

There are other issues here that I can write for the failing tests. Notice that if I were to provide a single observation and provide a set of observations, every assertion that I've listed so far would succeed. So, I write a new test to ensure that NumberGuesser guesses every number at least once. We can code this up in the following way:

```
def given_a_one_off_observation_followed_by_a_set_of_observations_
test():
    #given
    number_guesser = NumberGuesser()
    previously_chosen_numbers = [1,2]
    one_off_observation = 0
    all_observations = previously_chosen_numbers + [one_off_observation]
    number_guesser.number_was(one_off_observation)
    number_guesser.numbers_were(previously_chosen_numbers)
    #when
    guessed_numbers = [number_guesser.guess() for i in range(0,100)]
    #then
    for guessed_number in guessed_numbers:
      assert guessed_number in all_observations, 'every guess should
be one of the previously chosen numbers'
      assert len(set(guessed_numbers)) == len(all_observations), "It
should eventually guess every number at least once."
```

And my final code looks like the following:

```
import random

class NumberGuesser:
  """Guesses numbers based on the history of your input"""
  def __init__(self):
    self._guessed_numbers = []
  def numbers_were(self, guessed_numbers):
    self._guessed_numbers += guessed_numbers
  def number_was(self, guessed_number):
    self._guessed_numbers.append(guessed_number)
  def guess(self):
    if self._guessed_numbers == []:
      return None
    return random.choice(self._guessed_numbers)
```

Technically, there is a chance that this test will fail just due to a random chance. The probability of this test failing for this reason is 0.5^{100}, which is 7.9×10^{-31}. Basically, the chance is zero.

Different approaches to validating the improved models

Model quality validation, of course, depends upon the kinds of models that you're building, and the purpose of them. There are a few general types of machine learning problems that I've covered in this book, and each has different ways of validating model quality.

Classification overview

We'll get to the specifics in just a moment, but let's review the high-level terms. One method for quantifying the quality of a supervised classification is using ROC curves. These can be quantified by finding the total area under the curve (AUC), finding the location of the inflection point, or by simply setting a limit of the amount of data that must be classified correctly against percentage of the time.

Another common technique is that of a confusion matrix. Limits can be set on certain cells of the matrix to help drive testing. Also, they can be used as a diagnostic tool that can help identify the issues that come up.

We will typically use the k-fold cross validation. Cross validation is a technique where we take our sample dataset and divide it into several separate datasets. We can then use one of these datasets to develop against one of the others, to validate that our data isn't overfitted, and a third dataset for a final check to see whether the others went well. All of these separate datasets work to make sure that we develop a generally applicable model, and not just one that predicts our training data but falls apart in production.

Regression

Linear regression quality is typically quantified with the combination of an adjusted- $R2$ value and by checking this, the residuals of the model don't fit a pattern. How do we check for this in an automated test?

The adjusted $R2$ values are provided by the most statistical tools. It's a quick measure of how much of the variations in the data is explained by your model. Checking model assumptions is more difficult. It is much easier to see patterns visually than via discrete, specific tests.

So, this is hard but there are other tests… perhaps, even more important tests that are easier — cross-validation. By selecting strong test datasets with a litany of misbehavior, we can compare $R2$ statistics from development, to testing, to ready for production. If a serious drop occurs at any point, then we can circle back.

Clustering

Clustering is the way in which we create our classification model. From there, we can test it by cross validating against our data. This can be especially useful in clustering algorithms, such as k-means, where the feedback can help us tune the number of clusters we want to use to minimize the cluster variation. As we move from one cross-validation dataset to another, it's important to remember not to persist with our training data from the previous tests, lest we bias our results.

Quantifying the classification models

To make sure that we're on the same page, let's start by looking at an example of an ROC curve and the AUC score. The scikit-learn documentation has an example code to build an ROC curve and calculate AUC, which you can find at `http://scikit-learn.org/stable/auto_examples/model_selection/plot_roc.html`.

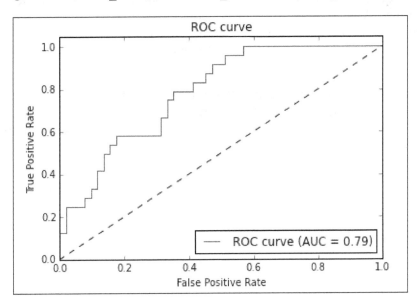

This ROC curve was built by running a classifier over the famous iris dataset. It shows us the true positive rate (*y*-axis) that we can get if we allow a given amount of false positive rate (*x*-axis). For example, if we were good with a 50 percent false positive rate, we would expect to see somewhere around a 90 percent true positive rate. Also, notice that the AUC percentage is 80 percent. Keeping in mind that a perfect classifier would score 100 percent, this seems pretty great. The dashed line in the chart represents a terrible and completely random (read non-predictive) model. An ideal model would be one that is pulled to the upper left-hand corner of the chart as much as possible. You can see in this chart that the model is somewhere between the two, which is pretty good. Whether or not that is acceptable depends on the problem that is being solved. How so?

Well, what if our classifier is attempting to identify the customers who would respond well to an advertisement? Every customer that we show it to who doesn't respond well to it has some chance of never doing business with us again. Let's say (though it's quite extreme) that the cost is so high that we need to eliminate all the false positives. Well, judging from our previous curve, this would mean we would only identify 10-15 percent of the true positives that exist. In this example, the little bit of performance boost is making more money, and so it's working quite well for our situation.

Imagine there's a one in 10,000 chance that if we incorrectly show a specific ad to someone, they'll sue us and it will cost us on average $25,000. Now, what does a good model look like? Here's a chart that I've created from the same previous ROC data, but with the following new set of parameters:

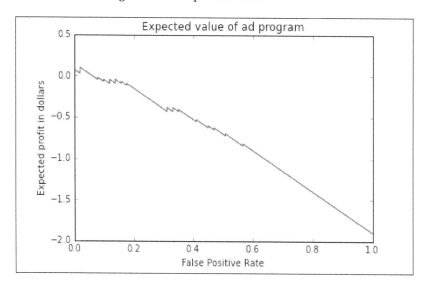

The maximum profit occurs right around a 1.9 percent false positive rate. As you can see, there is a huge drop off after that, even though this classifier works pretty well. For the purpose of this chapter, we can worry about writing the code for such thing as we progress. For now, it's fine to just have this gain chart. We'll get into guiding our process with these kind of results in future chapters.

Summary

In this chapter, you were introduced to TDD, as well as BDD. With these concepts introduced, you have a basic foundation with which to approach machine learning. We saw that specifying behavior in the form of sentences makes it easier to ready a set of specifications for your software.

Building off of that foundation, we started to delve into testing at a higher level. We did this by establishing concepts that we can use to quantify classifiers: the ROC curve and AUC metric. Now we've seen that different models can be quantified, it follows that they can be compared.

Putting all of this together, we have everything we need to explore machine learning with a test-driven methodology. In the next chapter, we will build a simple perceptron algorithm with TDD and measure its quality.

2
Perceptively Testing a Perceptron

Even for people comfortable with using them, neural networks can seem like a big black box. On top of that, the little bit of randomness within them just makes their inner workings that much more mysterious.

In this chapter, we're going to start exploring TDD-ing machine learning algorithms by building a very simple neural network using TDD. Then we will use this as an opportunity to more deeply understand how they work.

In this chapter, we will cover the following topics:

- Building the simplest perceptron possible
- Using a spreadsheet to develop simple use cases we can test to and reproduce
- Using TDD to develop our first machine-learning algorithm
- Testing with datasets

You will need some sort of spreadsheet program to follow along with this chapter. Microsoft Excel, Libre Office, or Google Docs are completely fine.

Getting started

A perceptron is a binary linear classifier. Like other supervised learning techniques, we can feed in rows of data along with the appropriate classification. After enough of these, the perceptron can begin to label new rows of data that have yet to be classified. Specifically, a perceptron works by adjusting a hyperplane to separate two groups of data as accurately as possible (with a linear classifier). Said a bit more simply, that means that we will have some data in a space and then perturb something like a line until it can act as an arbiter of what fits in one classification or another.

If you want to visualize it, think of 2D data being separated by a line like so:

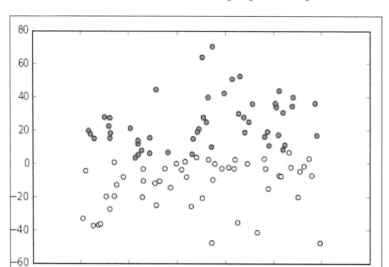

We'll be using TDD to develop the algorithm ourselves as an example of breaking very large problems down as much as possible. In later chapters, we will lean on third-party libraries for other implementations and focus on other ways to drive your machine learning forward in discrete steps.

It can be hard to figure out where to start creating a perceptron that doesn't include building the whole algorithm. We can start with a scenario that's so simple it's obviously not going to work. What's the value in a test like that? It gets us started. Let's get started with this:

```
def no_training_data_supplied_test():
    the_perceptron = Perceptron()
    result = the_perceptron.predict()
    nt.assert_none(result, 'Should have no result with no training
data.')
```

Getting this test to pass should be a pretty straightforward:

```
class Perceptron:
    def predict(self):
        return None
```

Doesn't get much simpler than that. Next we can try training the simplest possible case in the perceptron.

Keep in mind, we aren't doing test-driven math. It is perfectly okay to lean on the knowledge you have of the algorithms to inform the design of your code and the way you choose to get your tests to pass. In this case, you may like to take a step back and re-evaluate the math behind a simple perceptron and how to break it down into its simplest components.

One way to do this is to manually perform the math using a spreadsheet so that you can step through the calculations row by row. Here is an example of a pretty simple starting point:

	Training rate			0.25				
Iteration	Training 1	Training 2	Training label	Weights 1	Weights 2	Weight 1 update	Weight 2 update	Predicted value
1	1	1	1	0.96897982	0.97171753	0.968979818	0.971717531	1
1	1	0	1	0.96897982	0.97171753	0.968979818	0.971717531	1
1	0	1	1	0.96897982	0.97171753	0.968979818	0.971717531	1
1	0	0	0	0.96897982	0.97171753	0.968979818	0.971717531	0

Each row of the spreadsheet acts as a step through the training process for the perceptron. For the **Weights 1** and **Weights 2** columns, we can just make up some small random number. **Weight 1 update** and **Weight 2 update** are the values of the respective weights taking into account the training data. Mathematically stated, that means this (as defined in *Machine Learning: An Algorithmic Perspective*, Marsland):

$$w_{i+1,j} = w_{i,j} + \eta * w_{i,j} * \left(t_j - p_j \right)$$

This can be translated to normal speak as the updated weight is equal to that weight's current value plus the product of the training rate, the current weight, and the difference of the training value and the current pre-trained prediction value. Translated to Excel parlance we have this:

	A	B	C	D	E	F	G	H	I
1		Training rate		0.25					
2									
3	Iteration	Training 1	Training 2	Training label	Weights 1	Weights 2	Weight 1 update	Weight 2 update	Predicted value
4	1	1	1	1	0.96897982	0.97171753	=E4+D1*($D4-$I4)*B4		1

The weights in each subsequent row are updated based on the updated weights in the row immediately above. In this way, each row is incrementally tuning the weights of the perceptron.

Predicting the values (as done in the last column) is defined mathematically as:

$$p_j = \sum w_i * x_i > 0$$

Here, the output of the condition is 1 for true and 0 for false. In case a spreadsheet makes more sense to you, this is how that translates:

	A	B	C	D	E	F	G	H	I	J
1		Training rate		0.25						
2										
3	Iteration	Training 1	Training 2	Training label	Weights 1	Weights 2	Weight 1 update	Weight 2 update	Predicted value	
4	1	1	1	1	0.96897982	0.97171753	0.968979818	0.971717531	=IF((B4*E4+C4*F4)>0,1,0)	
5	1	1	0	1	0.96897982	0.97171753	0.968979818	0.971717531	1	
6	1	0	1	1	0.96897982	0.97171753	0.968979818	0.971717531	1	
7	1	0	0	0	0.96897982	0.97171753	0.968979818	0.971717531	0	

We could do several iterations as well by just repeating the rows. We will touch on that a bit later when we tackle something more complex. This scenario only requires one pass through the training data however. Really it only requires the first input in the training data since the weights don't seem to change in any of the rows after they're updated. We can use this fact to simplify what we test.

Let's write a test to capture this scenario:

```
def train_an_OR_function_test():
  the_perceptron = Perceptron([1,1],1)
  the_perceptron = Perceptron([1,0],1)
  the_perceptron = Perceptron([0,1],1)
  the_perceptron = Perceptron([0,0],1)
  nt.assert_equal(the_perceptron.predict([1,1]), 1)
  nt.assert_equal(the_perceptron.predict([1,0]), 1)
  nt.assert_equal(the_perceptron.predict([0,1]), 1)
  nt.assert_equal(the_perceptron.predict([0,0]), 0)
```

To solve this, your first pass may be to take what you learned from the Excel file and just apply it directly. Something like this:

```
class Perceptron:
  def __init__(self):
    self._weight_1 = 0.20
    self._weight_2 = 0.20
  def train(self, inputs, label):
    input = inputs[0]
    self._weight_1 = self._weight_1 + .25 * (input[0] - label[0]) *
self.predict(input)
    self._weight_2 = self._weight_2 + .25 * (input[1] - label[0]) *
self.predict(input)
  def predict(self, input):
    if len(input) == 0:
      return None
    return 0 < self._weight_1 * input[0] + self._weight_2 *
input[1]
```

You might realize… while this makes the tests pass, it's a fair bit of code. Maybe it could be simplified. In actuality, you can delete most of it and have the tests still pass, as shown:

```
class Perceptron:
  def __init__(self):
    self._weight_1 = 0.20
    self._weight_2 = 0.20
  def train(self, inputs, label):
    pass
  def predict(self, input):
    if len(input) == 0:
      return None
    return 0 < self._weight_1 * input[0] + self._weight_2 *
input[1]
```

This passes as well. It's much simpler and really is just an implementation of the prediction computation. For our scenario, the training process doesn't even matter. The training process is still included in the test though, because the fact that it doesn't make our tests pass is an implementation concern. As a user of the class, I would expect that the Perceptron would need training input. So let's leave that there for now even though the method feels superfluous.

Next, let's code a new scenario. Again, we will be choosing the next case based on our understanding of the algorithm. If you have a spreadsheet, explore simple scenarios that require you to tack on new complexity. Let's try making a perceptron that can signal when one or both of the outputs are positive. This is what a spreadsheet-based example might look like:

	A	B	C	D	E	F	G	H	I
1		Training rate		0.1					
2									
3	Iteration	Training 1	Training 2	Training label	Weights 1	Weights 2	Weight 1 update	Weight 2 update	Predicted value
4	1	5	-1	1	0.431	0.02	0.431	0.02	1
5	1	2	-1	0	0.431	0.02	0.231	0.12	1
6	1	0	-1	0	0.231	0.12	0.231	0.12	0
7	1	-2	-1	0	0.231	0.12	0.231	0.12	0
8	2	5	-1	1	0.231	0.12	0.231	0.12	1
9	2	2	-1	0	0.231	0.12	0.031	0.22	1
10	2	0	-1	0	0.031	0.22	0.031	0.22	0
11	2	-2	-1	0	0.031	0.22	0.031	0.22	0
12	3	5	-1	1	0.031	0.22	0.531	0.12	0
13	3	2	-1	0	0.531	0.12	0.331	0.22	1
14	3	0	-1	0	0.331	0.22	0.331	0.22	0
15	3	-2	-1	0	0.331	0.22	0.331	0.22	0
16	4	5	-1	1	0.331	0.22	0.331	0.22	1
17	4	2	-1	0	0.331	0.22	0.131	0.32	1
18	4	0	-1	0	0.131	0.32	0.131	0.32	0
19	4	-2	-1	0	0.131	0.32	0.131	0.32	0
20	5	5	-1	1	0.131	0.32	0.131	0.32	1
21	5	2	-1	0	0.131	0.32	0.131	0.32	0
22	5	0	-1	0	0.131	0.32	0.131	0.32	0
23	5	-2	-1	0	0.131	0.32	0.131	0.32	0

The spreadsheet is set up using the same formulas as last time. The first row handles setting initial values and each subsequent row refers to the previous row to get updated weights. Columns A-D are all inputs with each block of rows within a given iteration repeating in the next iteration. It's easiest to think of it repeating as a sort of loop.

Since we have an example scenario, let's use it to write our next test. This example is a little weird since it includes the use of a dummy variable and it requires several iterations to converge to the right solution. The use of a dummy variable allows our classifier to not be forced to be centered around 0. Essentially, it allows us to move the dividing line between true and false.

Since we already support two inputs, we're going to just include the dummy variable in our test for now so we can focus on getting the iteration working. Once that's stable, then we'll work at refactoring to include the dummy variable by default. The reason for separating these two needs is that if the updates break our other test, this will allow us to know that the iteration is what broke it instead of having two possible causes.

Here is a test case based upon the spreadsheet scenario:

```
def detect_values_greater_than_five_test():
  the_perceptron = Perceptron()
  the_perceptron.train([
                        [ 5, -1],
                        [ 2, -1],
                        [ 0, -1],
                        [-2, -1],
                       ],
                       [1,0,0,0])
  nt.assert_equal(the_perceptron.predict([ 8, -1]),   1)
  nt.assert_equal(the_perceptron.predict([ 5, -1]),   1)
  nt.assert_equal(the_perceptron.predict([ 2, -1]),   0)
  nt.assert_equal(the_perceptron.predict([ 0, -1]),   0)
  nt.assert_equal(the_perceptron.predict([-2, -1]),   0)
```

We can get the test to pass with the following code:

```
class Perceptron:
  def __init__(self):
    self._weight_1 = 0.431
    self._weight_2 = 0.02
  def train(self, inputs, labels):
    for _ in range(4):
```

```
        for input, label in zip(inputs, labels):
            label_delta = (label - self.predict(input))
            self._weight_1 = self._weight_1 + .1 * input[0] *
label_delta
            self._weight_2 = self._weight_2 + .1 * input[1] *
label_delta
    def predict(self, input):
        if len(input) == 0:
            return None
        return int(0 < self._weight_1 * input[0] + self._weight_2 *
input[1])
```

If you notice, in the constructor the weights are different from what they were. We do this so that our code matches our spreadsheet example exactly and we can make sure the code is doing exactly what our scenario did. This also helps us to choose a reasonable number of times to iterate over the weights so that everything will update.

In terms of refactoring, there are some opportunities here. The most important one is that we don't want to have to keep creating one off weight names and handling each input individually. We could refactor this and make it able to handle an unbounded number of inputs.

For the first step of this refactoring, let's focus on getting our weights to be array-based:

```
class Perceptron:
    def __init__(self):
        self._weights = [0.431, 0.02]
    def train(self, inputs, labels):
        for _ in range(4):
            for input, label in zip(inputs, labels):
                label_delta = (label - self.predict(input))
                self._weights[0] = self._weights[0] + .1 * input[0] *
label_delta
                self._weights[1] = self._weights[1] + .1 * input[1] *
label_delta
    def predict(self, input):
        if len(input) == 0:
            return None
        return int(0 < self._weights[0] * input[0] + self._weights[1]
* input[1])
```

Rerun the tests and ensure that they are still passing. Now we can refactor to handle *N* input variables. While we're at it (and to save page space), let's also refactor the weight updating to use += to make the code more succinct. This is the code with this update:

```
class Perceptron:
  def __init__(self):
    self._weights = [0.431, 0.02]
  def train(self, inputs, labels):
    for _ in range(4):
      for input, label in zip(inputs, labels):
        label_delta = (label - self.predict(input))
        for index, x in enumerate(input):
          self._weights[index] += .1 * x * label_delta
  def predict(self, input):
    if len(input) == 0:
      return None
    return int(0 < self._weights[0] * input[0] + self._weights[1]
* input[1])
```

Now, we can also move the initial weight definition into the train function. By doing this, we set ourselves up to generate the weights automatically based on the number of input variables we have. The final code for now is:

```
class Perceptron:
  def train(self, inputs, labels):
    self._weights = [0.431, 0.02]
    for _ in range(4):
      for input, label in zip(inputs, labels):
        label_delta = (label - self.predict(input))
        for index, x in enumerate(input):
          self._weights[index] += .1 * x * label_delta
  def predict(self, input):
    if len(input) == 0:
      return None
    return int(0 < self._weights[0] * input[0] + self._weights[1] *
input[1])
```

Next we will handle moving the dummy values of -1 into the perceptron. To do this, we will change the test we just finished by removing the negative ones. We will then get it to pass again by moving the negative ones into the Perceptron class itself:

```
def detect_values_greater_than_five_test():
  the_perceptron = Perceptron()
  the_perceptron.train([
```

```
                              [ 5,  -1],
                              [ 2,  -1],
                              [ 0,  -1],
                              [-2,  -1],
                          ],
                          [1,0,0,0])
    nt.assert_equal(the_perceptron.predict([ 8]),     1)
    nt.assert_equal(the_perceptron.predict([ 5]),     1)
    nt.assert_equal(the_perceptron.predict([ 2]),     0)
    nt.assert_equal(the_perceptron.predict([ 0]),     0)
    nt.assert_equal(the_perceptron.predict([-2]),     0)
```

Now when we run the test, we have an error that says list index out of range. We still have a hard-coded number of weights in the predict function. So we can fix that first. Here is the refactored predict function:

```
def predict(self, input):
  if len(input) == 0:
    return None
  weight_input_pairings = zip(self._weights, input)
  weight_input_products = [x[0]*x[1] for x in
weight_input_pairings]
  return int(0 < sum(weight_input_products))
```

Rerunning the test makes it fail for the right reason. At this point, we are ready to make it pass completely.

```
class Perceptron:
  def train(self, inputs, labels):
    self._weights = [0.431, 0.02, 0.2]
    dummied_inputs = [x + [-1] for x in inputs]
    for _ in range(4):
      for input, label in zip(dummied_inputs, labels):
        label_delta = (label - self.predict(input))
        for index, x in enumerate(input):
          self._weights[index] += .1 * x * label_delta
  def predict(self, input):
    if len(input) == 0:
      return None
    input = input + [-1]
    return int(0 < self._weights[0] * input[0] + self._weights[1]
* input[1])
```

On the first line of the training function, we cheat and hard code in an extra weight for the dummy variable. In the case of our first test, this weight ensures we will have enough weights after we add the dummy variable. For our most recent test, the extra weight will just be ignored since we only have one input.

We should refactor this so the code is generalized to apply to *N* inputs completely. It actually just requires a very small change in the code:

```
class Perceptron:
  def train(self, inputs, labels):
    dummied_inputs = [x + [-1] for x in inputs]
    self._weights = [0.2] * len(dummied_inputs[0])
    print(self._weights)
    for _ in range(4):
      for input, label in zip(dummied_inputs, labels):
        label_delta = (label - self.predict(input))
        for index, x in enumerate(input):
          self._weights[index] += .1 * x * label_delta
  def predict(self, input):
    if len(input) == 0:
      return None
    input = input + [-1]
    return int(0 < self._weights[0] * input[0] + self._weights[1]
* input[1])
```

We just auto-generate the weights based on the number of inputs we have (including the dummy input). In the literature for Neural Networks we are told that the weights should be randomly generated, but let's leave that alone for a bit since it hasn't caused us problems yet.

This next test will be a bit larger. We're going to randomly generate a fair amount of data to train the perceptron and then we're going to test it against some more randomly generated data. Our unit test will then make an assertion about a lower bound of how well the perceptron should work:

```
import numpy as np
def detect_a_complicated_example_test():
  # Create random variables
  n = 100
  inputs = map(list, zip(np.random.uniform(0,100,n),
      np.random.uniform(0,100,n),
      np.random.uniform(0,100,n)))
  labels = [int(x[0] + x[1] + x[2] < 150) for x in inputs]
  the_perceptron = Perceptron()
```

```
the_perceptron.train(inputs, labels)

n = 1000
test_inputs = map(list, zip(np.random.uniform(0,100,n),
    np.random.uniform(0,100,n),
    np.random.uniform(0,100,n)))
test_labels = [int(x[0] + x[1] + x[2] < 150) for x in
test_inputs]

# Create separate test cases
false_positives = 0
true_positives = 0
false_negatives = 0
true_negatives = 0
for input, label in zip(test_inputs, test_labels):
  prediction = the_perceptron.predict(input)
  if prediction == 1:
    if label == 1:
      true_positives += 1
    else:
      false_positives += 1
  else:
    if label == 0:
      true_negatives += 1
    else:
      false_negatives += 1
# Make sure we generated as much data as we'd expect
nt.assert_equal(false_positives+true_positives+true_negatives+false_
negatives, n)
correctly_classified = true_positives + true_negatives
assert correctly_classified > n*.9,   \
      "Perceptron should be much better than random. {0}
correct".format(correctly_classified)
```

When we first run this test, we have some issues. The first thing to notice is that the predict function still isn't generalized. This is why we chose to look at a three dimensional problem. If we generalized correctly, we shouldn't have to do anything to account for new variables. So first we change that. The updated predict method looks like this:

```
def predict(self, input):
  if len(input) == 0:
    return None
  input = input + [-1]
  return int(0 < sum([x[0]*x[1] for x in zip(self._weights,
input)]))
```

Now after running this again, the error changes. You may see something similar to the following:

```
=================================================================
FAIL: tests.detect_a_complicated_example_test
-----------------------------------------------------------------
Traceback (most recent call last):
  File "/Library/Python/2.7/site-packages/nose-1.3.0-py2.7.egg/nose/ca
se.py", line 197, in runTest
    self.test(*self.arg)
  File "/Users/justin/Documents/Code/test-driven-machine-learning/Chap
ter 2 Redux/tests.py", line 75, in detect_a_complicated_example_test
    "Perceptron should be much better than random. {0} correct".format
(correctly_classified)
AssertionError: Perceptron should be much better than random. 1367 cor
rect


-----------------------------------------------------------------
Ran 5 tests in 0.082s

FAILED (failures=1)
```

Our perceptron only managed to classify 1,367 out of 2,500 inputs correctly. That is basically no better than random. The first thing we should start thinking about is what aspect of the theory we have avoided up until now? The one we discussed just before this test was the number of iterations. We currently only make our perceptron iterate four times and we noted that it seemed like a rather tiny limit. From here we can experiment with different values to see what works with the lowest running time. The following is a chart that shows how many correct predictions the perceptron got in a trial run with varying numbers of iterations:

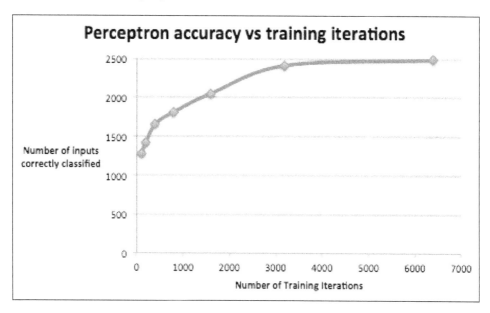

Using this chart, we can see that ~2,500 iterations will give us a pretty good idea that we're getting better than random results.

Summary

In this chapter, we iteratively developed the foundation of a neural network (a perceptron) using TDD by first developing concrete scenarios in a spreadsheet. Using a spreadsheet allowed us to get a handle on each of the different calculations that are required in a perceptron. We also saw that we can use TDD without needing to prove the mathematics. Instead we used TDD to implement the smallest amount of the mathematics that we needed to make our perceptron perform incrementally better. A side benefit to this is that you may have also developed a deeper understanding of what each aspect of the perceptron actually does.

In the next chapter, we will continue exploring mathematical solutions to machine learning. Specifically, we will develop a solution to maximize the money we can make when we have several different options of what to show customers and have no idea which is the most profitable.

3

Exploring the Unknown with Multi-armed Bandits

We'll start this chapter by building a simplistic algorithm and measuring its quality. Next, we'll build a much more intelligent algorithm. We will also build some tests to measure the quality improvement that we will achieve, specifically, a **multi-armed bandit** algorithm.

Understanding a bandit

A multi-armed bandit problem involves making a choice in the face of complete uncertainty. More specifically, imagine you're placed in front of several slot machines, and each has a different but fixed probability to pay out. How could you make as much money as possible?

So, this is a metaphor for the problem. It really applies to any situation where you have no information to start with, and where you stand to gain something.

There are two concepts that are critical in understanding algorithms that solve this class of problem: **exploration** and **exploitation**. Exploration refers to the algorithm choosing to play a strategy to gain more information about the given strategy. Exploitation is what happens when the algorithm decides to try the currently winning strategy in an effort to maximize the pay off. A great concrete example of this is split testing (or A/B testing), which is a feature on a website. Imagine an algorithm that only ever chooses the current best-performing strategy. It's conceivable that this algorithm may fall into a rut and only ever try one strategy. This is extremely sub-optimal, since there is no way that the algorithm can break out of this rut as long as the one strategy continues to perform better than the other strategies have up to this point.

Say, you are tasked with improving visitor searching on your home page, and you have a couple of ideas for a headline to entice them. Let's say that there is a pre-existing headline (treatment A), and we have two additional choices (treatment B and C). If you were to try and decide which treatment to show to the visitors, how would you do it? Here's one solution (albeit quite naïve and suboptimal):

1. Show each one of the treatments to 100 visitors. This is the exploration phase.

2. Compute the percent of visitors who have searched it.

3. Next, show the treatment that had the highest percentage to the next 100 visitors. This is the exploitation phase.

4. Now, go to step number 1.

Again, this is completely sub-optimal, but it serves to illustrate the idea.

Testing with simulation

A recurring theme in this book is to use what's known as **Monte Carlo** methods to quantify the quality of our algorithm. Using this technique, we will time and again create groups of random data to see how well our algorithms (ignorant of how we created the data) perform at detecting the differences. In the previous chapter, most of the tests that we developed had deterministic test cases. In this chapter, the test cases will be specified by the parameters that we use, but all of the data that we create will be random.

First things first, we need to develop a small framework that we can use to run our simulations. In order to do this, we should more clearly articulate our scenario. Here's a more thorough definition.

Imagine we have a website, and we want to test three different treatments of the headline on it. We decide to run a test by randomly assigning every visitor to one of the three treatments. Our goal is to exploit our three treatments by figuring out which headline performs the best so that we can use it as much as possible. A simplifying assumption that we will make is that the probability of the given treatment that leads to a search is fixed across our population. We will also assume that the probability of each treatment that causes a visitor to search doesn't change overtime.

We won't build here in detail the simulation code that we will use to drive our tests.

Starting from scratch

To begin with, let's start building an extremely simplistic bandit algorithm. The actual bandit class will have two methods: `choose_treatment` and `log_payout`. The first method will recommend the best treatment to choose, and `log_payout` will be used to report back on how effective the recommended treatment was.

The simplest way to approach this algorithm from a test-driven perspective is to start with a single treatment so that the algorithm only has one thing to recommend. The code for this test looks like the following:

```
from nose.tools import assert_equal
import simple_bandit

def given_a_single_treatment_test():
  bandit = simple_bandit.SimpleBandit(['A'])
  chosen_treatment = bandit.choose_treatment()
  assert_equal(chosen_treatment, 'A', 'Should choose the only
available option.')
```

Again, we'll start from such a simple place that making the test pass will seem too easy:

```
class SimpleBandit:
  def __init__(self, treatments):
    self._treatments = treatments
  def choose_treatment(self):
    return self._treatments[0]
```

Since this first bandit algorithm will be purposefully simple, the next test will instruct the algorithm to start the exploration with the first treatment in its list:

```
def given_two_treatments_and_no_payoffs_test():
  treatments = ['A','B']
  bandit = simple_bandit.SimpleBandit(treatments)
  chosen_treatment = bandit.choose_treatment()
  assert_equal(chosen_treatment, treatments[0], 'Should choose the
first treatment to start')
```

As you might expect, this test passes right off. Next, let's focus on getting through the exploration phase. For this simple algorithm, let's try each treatment five times, and then choose the one with the highest pay off for five times. After this, let's go back and explore another five times per treatment. We'll just choose some naïve strategy; there's nothing special about this one, but it works as a starting point. First, we'll make sure that the algorithm chooses treatment A five times:

```
def given_two_treatments_test():
  treatments = ['A','B']
  bandit = simple_bandit.SimpleBandit(treatments)
  treatments_chosen = []
  for i in range(5):
    chosen_treatment = bandit.choose_treatment()
    treatments_chosen.append(chosen_treatment)
  assert_equal(treatments_chosen.count('A', 5, 'Should explore
treatment A for the first 5 tries')
```

Then, we'll have the algorithm choose five more treatments. They should all be B. Let's make the previous test look like the following one now:

```
def given_two_treatments_test():
  treatments = ['A','B']
  bandit = simple_bandit.SimpleBandit(treatments)
  treatments_chosen = []
  for i in range(5):
    chosen_treatment = bandit.choose_treatment()
    treatments_chosen.append(chosen_treatment)
  assert_equal(treatments_chosen.count('A'), 5, 'Should explore
treatment A for the first 5 tries')

  for i in range(5):
    chosen_treatment = bandit.choose_treatment()
    treatments_chosen.append(chosen_treatment)
  assert_equal(treatments_chosen.count('B'), 5, 'Should explore
treatment B for the next 5 tries')
```

We can get the latter half of this test working with the following code:

```
class SimpleBandit:
  def __init__(self, treatments):
    self._treatments = treatments
    self._selection_count = 0
  def choose_treatment(self):
    self._selection_count += 1
    return self._treatments[(self._selection_count-1) / 5]
```

We can cheat and just use integer division to make sure we loop through each iteration and try each one at least five times. Now we get to the part where we make the algorithm start to exploit what it knows to be the best option. The implementation of this test looks as follows:

```
def given_two_treatments_test():
  treatments = ['A','B']
  bandit = simple_bandit.SimpleBandit(treatments)
  treatments_chosen = []
  for i in range(5):
    chosen_treatment = bandit.choose_treatment()
    treatments_chosen.append(chosen_treatment)
    bandit.log_payout(chosen_treatment, 0.00)
  assert_equal(treatments_chosen.count('A'), 5, 'Should explore
treatment A for the first 5 tries')

  for i in range(5):
    chosen_treatment = bandit.choose_treatment()
    treatments_chosen.append(chosen_treatment)
    bandit.log_payout(chosen_treatment, 5.00)
  assert_equal(treatments_chosen.count('B'), 5, 'Should explore
treatment B for the next 5 tries')

  for i in range(5):
    chosen_treatment = bandit.choose_treatment()
    treatments_chosen.append(chosen_treatment)
  assert_equal(treatments_chosen.count('B'), 10, 'Should explore
treatment B for the next 5 tries after exploring')
```

We'll log no payout for treatment. Thus, the algorithm will opt to keep with treatment B after the second round of exploration. We can make this pass with a slightly more complex class. This isn't perfect yet, but it's getting us to where we want to be:

```
class SimpleBandit:
  def __init__(self, treatments):
    self._treatments = treatments
    self._selection_count = 0
    self._payouts = {treatment: 0 for treatment in treatments}
  def choose_treatment(self):
    self._selection_count += 1
    if self._selection_count < 5*len(self._treatments):
      return self._treatments[(self._selection_count-1) / 5]
    else:
      return  max(self._payouts.items(), key=lambda x: x[1])[0]
  def log_payout(self, treatment, amount):
    self._payouts[treatment] += amount
```

At the very end of the test, add the last assert that the algorithm returned back to exploring, starting with the first treatment. In making the test pass, note that the previous code, at the sixth line from the bottom (in bold), should be slightly different. Here's the full code:

```
class SimpleBandit:
  def __init__(self, treatments):
    self._treatments = treatments
    self._selection_count = 0
    self._exploitation_count = 0
    self._payouts = {treatment: 0 for treatment in treatments}
  def choose_treatment(self):
    self._selection_count += 1
    if self._selection_count <= 5*len(self._treatments):
      return self._treatments[(self._selection_count-1) / 5]
    else:
      self._exploitation_count += 1
      if self._exploitation_count == 5:
        self._exploitation_count = 0
        self._selection_count = 0
      return sorted(self._payouts.items(), key=lambda x: x[1],
reverse=True)[0][0]
  def log_payout(self, treatment, amount):
    self._payouts[treatment] += amount
```

With this, we have our simple bandit built up. Next, we will test how it performs in our simulation. After this, we will move to building a bandit using a very different approach, and we will see where it gets us.

Simulating real world situations

What I'd like to do now is take a detour to see what the performance of this algorithm looks like over time. We won't be test driving the simulation harness that I will use here. We will instead use this as an opportunity to visually identify the performance characteristics of two separate multi-armed bandit algorithms. Let's start introducing the different concepts from the code. The following code sets up our experimental world to be simulated. I'll instantiate BanditScenario and set up treatments A-C to have certain parameters that will provide guidance on how well each does in our experiment:

```
simulated_experiment = BanditScenario({
  'A': {
    'conversion_rate': .05,
    'order_average': 35.00
```

```
    },
    'B':{
      'conversion_rate': .06,
      'order_average': 36.00
    }
  })
```

The code should be read as *The probability of treatment A causing a visitor to convert is 5 percent. If they order, the average order amount will be for $35.00*, and so on. The `BanditScenario` handles drawing random numbers as well as tracking the results. However, it logs in about what would have happened in each treatment, as well as what would have happened in the particular path that we chose. Let's look at how this ties together with our algorithm from the earlier section, and maybe then it will make more sense to you:

```
simple_bandit = SimpleBandit(['A', 'B'])

for visitor_i in range(500):
  treatment = simple_bandit.choose_treatment()
  payout = simulated_experiment.next_visitor(treatment)
  simple_bandit.log_payout(treatment, payout)

plt.title('Money made by different strategies')
plt.xlabel('Visitor #')
plt.ylabel('Total $ made')

plt.title('Money made by different strategies')
plt.xlabel('Visitor #')
plt.ylabel('Total $ made')

plt.plot(np.array(simulated_experiment._bandit_payoffs).
cumsum(),label='Bandit')
plt.plot(np.array(simulated_experiment._scenario_payoffs['B']).
cumsum(), label='Treatment B')
plt.plot(np.array(simulated_experiment._scenario_payoffs['A']).
cumsum(), label='Treatment A')
plt.legend(bbox_to_anchor=(1.05, 1), loc=2, borderaxespad=0.)
```

First, we instantiate our `SimpleBandit`, and provide it the name of every treatment in our experiment so that it can tell us which treatment to apply to our website and when. Next, we pretend each visit to our site happens sequentially, one right after another: 500 visitors in total. For each visitor, we'll have a simple bandit propose a treatment to show them by calling `choose_treatment`.

Then, the `simulated_experiment` will tell us what the payout was for that treatment `next_visitor` on `bandit_scenario`. With this, the scenario returns with the amount of money that we made from the visitor, which we'll then pass back into the `simple_bandit`. We do this so that it can learn and improve its ability to make money later. After all of this, we will generate a graph to help us visualize the differences. The graph looks as follows:

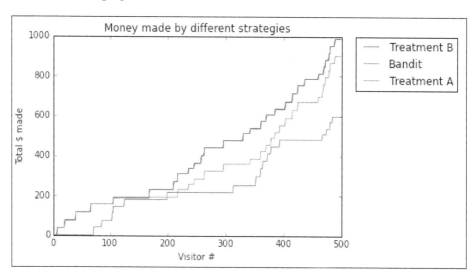

Wow! What's going on here? Well, the top line (also known as **Treatment B**) is pretty easy to explain. Treatment B has a 6 percent chance of converting a visitor, and it makes more money in each conversion. As a result, its cumulative payoff is almost always greater than the other two possible strategies. **Treatment A** has a lower chance of converting a visitor, and it makes less money when its visitors order, so, it's the worst treatment. True to the design, our `SimpleBandit` class learns which treatment to copy and by the end of the period, it has a cumulative payoff of almost that of our best treatment. If one magically knew that Treatment B was the best, then the top line would represent how well they could do so. To put it another way, it's our ideal maximum. Treatment A is our minimum or worst case (the lowest line). As you might expect, our bandit algorithm performs somewhere in between the two. For this simple algorithm, the performance varies wildly from run to run. Let's move on to a much more robust algorithm and see how it performs.

A randomized probability matching algorithm

The **randomized probability matching bandit** algorithm is a Bayesian statistical approach to the problem of figuring out when to explore our options and when to exploit them for a nice payoff. It works by sampling a probability distribution that describes the probable mean of the payoff. As we gain more data, the variance of the possible means narrows significantly. As we go through the rest of this chapter, we'll delve deeper into how this algorithm works.

As a concrete example, we can run some simulations. The following is a histogram of repeatedly sampling means with 100 samples from a normal distribution:

```
plt.title('Distribution of means for N(35,5) distribution (sampling
100 vs 500 data points)')
plt.xlabel('')
plt.ylabel('Counts')

plt.hist([np.random.normal(loc=35, scale=5, size=100).mean() for i in
range(2500)], label='100 sample mean')
plt.hist([np.random.normal(loc=35, scale=5, size=500).mean() for i in
range(2500)], label='500 sample mean')
plt.legend(bbox_to_anchor=(1.05, 1), loc=2, borderaxespad=0.)
```

And this is the chart the code generates:

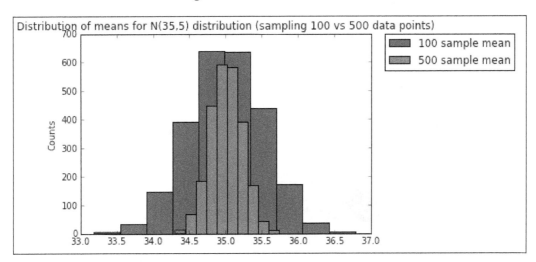

What this means is that if we were to sample a mean from the distribution where we have means of 500 data point samples, we are more likely to sample a mean closer to what it actually is. In this algorithm, what we do is pull a sample from a distribution that represents our current uncertainty of each variation. To simplify things a bit, let's not worry too much about the variance. If you're not too sure about how having a different variance can change the illustration, take a moment to experiment with the previous code. To illustrate how the number of data points influences our distribution, here is an example of our uncertainty of a normal mean of $34, versus a normal mean of $35 with only 50 data points:

```
plt.title('Distributions of a mean of 34 and 35 with 50 samples')
plt.xlabel('')
plt.ylabel('Counts')

plt.hist([np.random.normal(loc=35, scale=5, size=50).mean()
          for i in range(2500)],
          bins=30, label='mean of 35', alpha=.8)
plt.hist([np.random.normal(loc=34, scale=5, size=50).mean()
          for i in range(2500)],
          bins=30, label='mean of 34', alpha=.8)
plt.legend(bbox_to_anchor=(1.05, 1), loc=2, borderaxespad=0.)
```

The previous code generates the following chart:

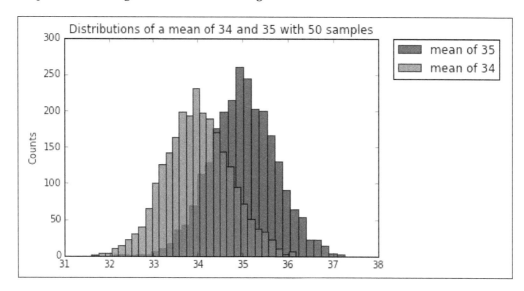

You can see it's quite possible to sometimes draw a sample out of the distribution that represents a higher mean, but let it be lesser than a sample that you draw from the distribution of the lower mean. How often? We can simulate this as well:

```
sum([np.random.normal(loc=34, scale=5, size=50).mean() >
np.random.normal(loc=35, scale=5, size=50).mean()
 for i in range(1500)])/1500.
```

If you run this code in your Python shell, you will get an answer approximately 15 percent of the time. So, when we only have 50 samples, this bandit algorithm might try out the treatment that seems worse around 15 percent of the time. This is quite different from our previous algorithm, which gave a fixed number of attempts, regardless of our uncertainty.

Let's start coding it and see how it performs against the other.

A bootstrapping bandit

Now, let's move to implement a simple approach that will use what we've been exploring. A bootstrapping bandit requires no math knowledge at all. It just requires us to sample from the data that we've encountered. Due to this simplicity, we can start from here. Let's start with the simplest test, as follows:

```
import rpm_bandit

def given_a_single_treatment_test():
  bandit = rpmbandit.RPMBandit(['A'])
  chosen_treatment = bandit.choose_treatment()
  assert chosen_treatment == 'A', 'Should choose the only
available option.'
```

Okay, it's pretty standard at this point. The code that I've written to make this pass is also pretty standard now:

```
class RPMBandit:
  def __init__(self, treatments):
    self._treatments = treatments
  def choose_treatment(self):
    return self._treatments[0]
```

Next, let's say we have two treatments and neither of them have any data yet. Let's make sure to choose one. I'm totally fine with always choosing the first one:

```
def given_a_multiple_treatment_test():
  bandit = rpm_bandit.RPMBandit(['A', 'B'])
  chosen_treatment = bandit.choose_treatment()
  assert chosen_treatment == 'A', 'Should choose first available
option.'
```

This just works without any changes.

Now, we can start getting down to brass tacks. Let the next test be that we have two treatments and one data sample for each one. It shouldn't always pick the one with the best value to try next. It should be randomized:

```
def given_a_multiple_treatment_with_a_single_sample_test():
  bandit = rpm_bandit.RPMBandit(['A', 'B'])
  bandit.log_payout('A', 35)
  bandit.log_payout('B', 34)

  treatment_a_chosen_count = sum([bandit.choose_treatment() == 'A'
for i in range(50)])
  assert treatment_a_chosen_count < 50, "Each treatment should be
assigned randomly"
```

We can fix this test by allowing the bandit to randomly choose a treatment, such as the following:

```
import random

class RPMBandit:
  def __init__(self, treatments):
    self._treatments = treatments
  def choose_treatment(self):
    return random.choice(self._treatments)
  def log_payout(self, treatment, payout):
    pass
```

The only issue is that this breaks our other test, because it always has to choose the first option. We can fix this, as follows:

```
def given_a_multiple_treatment_test():
  bandit = rpm_bandit.RPMBandit(['A', 'B'])
  chosen_treatment = bandit.choose_treatment()
  assert chosen_treatment in ['A', 'B'], 'Should choose first
available option.'
```

The next tests are going to get a bit more difficult. We may want to jump directly to the meat of the algorithm. Let's see if we can write this test:

```
def given_a_multiple_treatment_with_data_weighing_towards_a_treatment_
test():
  bandit = rpm_bandit.RPMBandit(['A', 'B'])
  bandit.log_payout('A', 100)
  bandit.log_payout('A', 120)
  bandit.log_payout('A', 150)
  bandit.log_payout('B', 34)
  bandit.log_payout('B', 35)
  bandit.log_payout('B', 32)
  treatment_a_chosen_count = sum([bandit.choose_treatment() == 'A'
for i in range(1000)])
  assert treatment_a_chosen_count > 900, 'Treatment A should be
chosen much more than 50% of the time.'
```

Here, we can see that A really begins to dominate early in the test. The relative difference in A's performance versus B's performance is night and day. Also, this test will cause us to get away from doing a simple random sample to doing something a bit fancier:

```
import random
import numpy as np
from collections import defaultdict

class RPMBandit:
  def __init__(self, treatments):
    self._treatments = treatments
    self._payoffs = {treatment: [] for treatment in treatments}
  def choose_treatment(self):
    max_treatment = self._treatments[0]
    max_value = float('-inf')
    for key, value in self._payoffs.items():
      sampled_mean = np.random.choice(value, size=len(value)).mean()
      if sampled_mean > max_value:
        max_treatment = key
        max_value = sampled_mean
    return max_treatment
  def log_payout(self, treatment, payout):
    self._payoffs[treatment].append(payout)
```

Oof. I added a fair amount of code to get this working, but now let me break another test in the mean time. The new approach is to utilize a bootstrap to deal with the approximation of a posterior distribution of the mean of our data. Even so, suddenly the algorithm begins to always choose the highest value treatment when there is only one sample available. I have an idea for fixing this. And it requires doing something less than savory:

```python
import random
import numpy as np

class RPMBandit:
  def __init__(self, treatments):
    self._treatments = treatments
    self._payoffs = {treatment: [] for treatment in treatments}
  def choose_treatment(self):
    max_treatment = self._treatments[0]
    max_value = float('-inf')
    for key, value in self._payoffs.items():
      random_numbers_from_range = np.random.binomial(len(value)+1,
1.0/(len(value)+1))
      generated_data = value + [random.uniform(0,200) for i in
range(random_numbers_from_range)]
      sampled_mean = np.random.choice(generated_data,
size=len(generated_data)).mean()
      if sampled_mean > max_value:
        max_treatment = key
        max_value = sampled_mean
    return max_treatment
  def log_payout(self, treatment, payout):
    self._payoffs[treatment].append(payout)
```

This gets my tests to pass. Let's explore why.

The problem with straight bootstrapping

What you could see happening was that with a single observation of data, bootstrapping will give the same answer every time. Ironically, this means that when you're bootstrapping such a small dataset, you will have zero variance. Here's an example in code:

```python
plt.hist([np.random.choice([1]) for i in range(100)])
```

The histogram for sampling from a dataset that consists of only one element looks as follows:

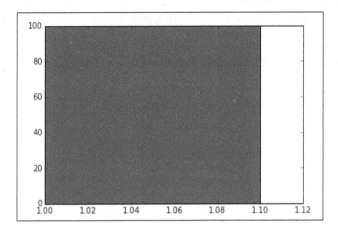

As predicted, every value is the same. This doesn't really match our intuition about uncertainty though. We have only observed a single number, but it could have just as easily been a different number. This technique doesn't capture it right now. So, how can we fix this? By throwing in a random number of course! It's not terribly academic, but hopefully the tests will reveal that the performance will farewell. Here's the same scenario with the improved bootstrap:

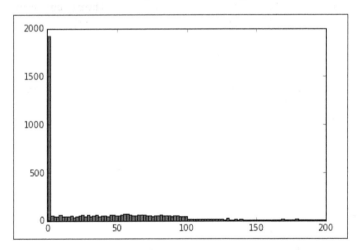

As you can see in this visualization, rather than all of the distribution being focused in a single bin, the distribution is spread out much more evenly. Even so, it's still incredibly focused. It's good enough to allow the algorithm to explore and work consistently, regardless of sample size.

Multi-armed armed bandit throw down

To compare the two algorithms, we're going to build a distribution that represents the payoffs of each algorithm, and do a quick test to see if the **RPMBandit** is, in fact, better than the **SimpleBandit** algorithm.

The following is a simulation harness that I've built to compare the two:

```python
def run_bandit_sim(bandit_algorithm):
    simulated_experiment = BanditScenario({
      'A': {
        'conversion_rate': 1,
        'order_average': 35.00
      },
      'B':{
        'conversion_rate': 1,
        'order_average': 50.00
      }
    })

    simple_bandit = bandit_algorithm

    for visitor_i in range(500):
      treatment = simple_bandit.choose_treatment()
      payout = simulated_experiment.next_visitor(treatment)
      simple_bandit.log_payout(treatment, payout)

    return sum(simulated_experiment._bandit_payoffs)

simple_bandit_results = np.array([run_bandit_sim(SimpleBandit(['A',
'B'])) for i in range(300)])
rpm_bandit_results = np.array([run_bandit_sim(RPMBandit(['A', 'B']))
for i in range(300)])

print 'SimpleBandit: ' + str(mean(simple_bandit_results))
print 'RPMBandit: ' + str(mean(rpm_bandit_results))

plt.title('Payoffs of SimpleBandit vs RPMBandit')
plt.xlabel('Total Payoff')
plt.ylabel('Observations')
plt.hist(simple_bandit_results, label='SimpleBandit', alpha=.8,
bins=40)
plt.hist(rpm_bandit_results, label='RPMBandit', alpha=.8, bins=40)
plt.legend(bbox_to_anchor=(1.05, 1), loc=2, borderaxespad=0.)
```

Using this, we can generate a graph similar to the following:

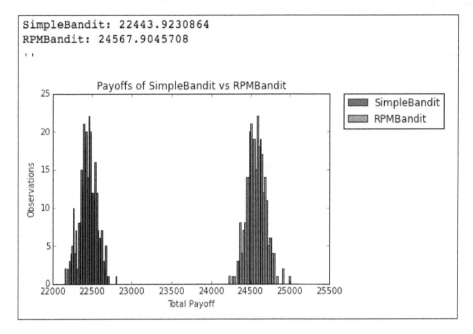

It's a night and day difference (almost a 10 percent increase). The distributions of the means of the two strategies don't even overlap. Given that, we can safely say that the RPM algorithm outperforms the Simple algorithm. I've noticed from playing with different settings that the less difference there is between the two treatment, the less the algorithm at hand matters. Then, something to take away is that a good multi-armed bandit algorithm will buffer you from the impact of extremely underperforming decisions, and encourage the overperforming decisions.

One last thing, let's convert the previous results into a test that we can use to guide the future algorithm selection. Here's a simple test that uses the simulation framework to test RPMBandit against SimpleBandit:

```
def run_comparison_test():
  simple_bandit_results = np.array([run_bandit_sim(simple_bandit.
SimpleBandit(['A', 'B']))
for i in range(300)])
  rpm_bandit_results = np.array([run_bandit_sim(rpm_bandit.
RPMBandit(['A', 'B'])) for i
in range(300)])
  rpm_better_count = sum(map(lambda x: x[0] > x[1], zip(rpm_bandit_
results, simple_bandit_results)))
  assert rpm_better_count/300. > .8, 'The RPM bandit should be
better at least 80% of the time.'
```

Summary

In this chapter, we **TDD**ed a simple and more complex algorithm, and then built a larger test to run the comparative benchmarking. The final comparative test ran slowly, which is less than ideal, but it could be improved by optimizing the algorithms for efficiency. You were also introduced to viewing histograms as probability distributions that can be viewed for feedback on how well our algorithm is doing. Last but not least, you learned how to create a bootstrapping approach to multi-armed bandit problems.

In the next chapter, we will dive into linear regression, and we will begin to integrate third-party libraries such as scipy into our TDD practice.

4
Predicting Values with Regression

In this chapter, we'll cover multiple linear regression and how to approach it from a TDD perspective. Unlike the previous chapters, where we developed the actual algorithm using TDD, in this chapter we will explore using a third-party library for the algorithm and TDD building our model. In order to do this, we'll need to find a way to quantify model quality as well as to quantify model assumption violations. We won't have the liberty of checking a data visualization to ensure that our model fits our criteria well.

We will also be using the Python packages `statsmodels` and `pandas`, so install those before moving forward in the chapter, using the following commands;

```
> pip install pandas
> pip install statsmodels
```

To start off, let's refresh ourselves on multiple regression and the key topics we'll need to drive us toward an excellent model.

Refresher on advanced regression

Before we get down to brass tacks on how we will tackle building regression models using TDD, we need to refresh ourselves on some of the finer points. Multiple regression comes packed with some assumptions and different measures of model quality. A good amount of this information can be found in *A Second Course in Statistics Regression Analysis, Mendenhall & Sincich, Pearson* (2011).

Regression assumptions

When a lot of people are introduced to regression, their main take-away is this is how we draw a line through our data to predict what it will be. To be fair, that's pretty accurate, but there's a fair amount of nuance in this that we need to explicitly discuss.

First let's discuss the standard multiple regression model form. It looks like this:

$$y = \beta_0 + \beta_1 x_1 + \beta_2 x_2 + \cdots + \beta_n x_n + \varepsilon$$

Here y is our dependent variable. Every x variable is an independent variable. y being a dependent variable means it is dependent on the values of the independent variables and the error term ε. The error term is so important because it means we can say that this model is completely correct for any specific set of values of x, since we can just add some constant ε to give us the correct result. Dealing with many sets of values for x is where we need to define some new assumptions.

One key assumption is that the errors in the model represented by the error term (also known as the residuals) are normally distributed. Why is that important? By assuming our residuals are normally distributed, it allows us to reliably specify confidence intervals for our predictions. In addition to this, we hold an assumption that the variance in our residuals will remain constant across observations.

When interpreting our models, keep in mind that for any x_i, the associated β_i is the slope of the line if all of the other x values remain fixed/constant. When developing our model, it is these slopes that we are attempting to estimate.

Quantifying model quality

There are a few different techniques we can use to establish quality. They help us determine whether a model is adequate, how well it explains the variation in our dependent variable (y in our case), and how much our different model parameters (our β_i values) contribute to understanding our data.

To test that our model is somewhat adequate, our first test is known as an **F-test**. The F-test checks that we have enough evidence to discard the null hypothesis that all of our beta values are equal to 0. If we aren't able to reject our null hypothesis, then we should rethink our model, perhaps by introducing interaction terms or other effects. This is one quantity we will want to test for.

After we've established that our model passes the F-test, then we can look at tuning our model and improving our results. To do this, we don't just seek to improve the p-value of our F-test; instead we can leverage a metric known as **Adjusted** R^2 aka R_a^2 or the **multiple coefficient of determination**. This number will range anywhere between 0 and 1. It is the percentage of the sample variance that our model explains. A value of 1 would mean that our model is a perfect fit while a value of 0 would mean our model explains none of the variation in our sampled data.

Another tool we have at our disposal is the **t-statistic** for each parameter in our model, which indicates how significantly our beta coefficients differs from zero. As we're looking for possible areas of our model to improve, we can look at the **t-statistic** for each β_i. If they are exceptionally small (identified by a **p-value** > 0.05 usually), this may be a sign we could improve our model by removing the parameter or changing it somehow. It's advisable to change only one parameter at a time because it can have significant impact on our other terms, making what were poor fits better fits and vice-versa.

The last thing that we'll cover is quantifying the normality of the residuals to validate our model assumptions. There are several techniques to do this. One qualitative technique is known as a **Q-Q Plot**. If our residuals are normally distributed, a **Q-Q Plot** will look like a straight line. That doesn't help us to quantify the assumption however.

A fairly straightforward way of quantifying how well the residuals fit the normality assumptions imposed by our model is the **Jarque-Bera test.** This test works by testing if the skewness and kurtosis likely come from a normally distributed distribution. The library we'll be using will compute it for us (along with many of these other metrics) automatically whenever we fit a model.

Of course, regression analysis is an extremely deep topic and there's more that we could verify, such as heteroscedasticity, but we'll stop here. Just know that if there's an aspect of your model you want to test, you can quantify it. Somehow.

Generating our own data

When exploring machine learning algorithms, it can be quite helpful to generate your own data. This gives you complete control and allows for the most exploration of a new technique you might try. It also lets you build trust that your model is working as planned given your assumptions. You've seen this multiple times already in this book up to this point, so it's nothing new. As we develop a linear regression model however, it will be even more instructive since I'm going to work backward through the example.

I will generate data first but show you how I generated the data at the end of the chapter. The goal here is to give you the opportunity to work through building a complex model from a statistical test-first perspective and ultimately show how the generating function was defined and how that affected our work.

The generated data is in the GitHub repo for this book (`https://github.com/jcbozonier/Machine-Learning-Test-by-Test`) so that you can follow along with the chapter.

Building the foundations of our model

Let's start by pulling the model into Python and transforming it into a form that we can use. To do this, we will need two additional libraries. We will use Pandas to read from our generated CSV and statsmodel to run our statistical procedures. Both libraries are pretty powerful and full of features, and we will only be touching on a few of them so feel free to explore them further later.

To start off, let's make a test that will run a simple regression over one of the variables and show us the output. That should give us a good place to start. I'm keeping this in a unit testing structure because I know I want to test this code and just want to explore a bit to know exactly what to test for. This first step you could do in a one-off file, but I'm choosing to start with it so I can build from it:

```
import pandas
import statsmodels.formula.api as sm
import nose.tools as nt

def vanilla_model_test():
    df = pandas.read_csv('./generated_data.csv')
    model_fit = sm.ols('dependent_var ~ ind_var_d', data=df).fit()
    print(model_fit.summary())
    assert False
```

If you're familiar with R, the `ols` fit syntax is probably pretty familiar and you can skip the next few sentences. The `ols` function requires two inputs: the regression formula to use and the data to pull from. In this syntax, the ~ essentially acts as an equals sign. The syntax in the function translates to the following:

$$dependent\_var = \beta_0 + \beta_1 * ind\_var\_d + \varepsilon$$

Our having a β_0 is assumed, so we don't need to explicitly declare it. The fact that we're using ind_var_d also automatically implies that there will be a beta coefficient for that variable. Finally, the error term is assumed as well.

From running this, we get the following summary printed out when we hit the assert False statement:

```
                          OLS Regression Results
==============================================================================
Dep. Variable:          dependent_var   R-squared:                       0.005
Model:                            OLS   Adj. R-squared:                 -0.030
Method:                 Least Squares   F-statistic:                    0.1499
Date:                Thu, 19 Feb 2015   Prob (F-statistic):              0.702
Time:                        20:57:08   Log-Likelihood:                -222.90
No. Observations:                  30   AIC:                             449.8
Df Residuals:                      28   BIC:                             452.6
Df Model:                           1
Covariance Type:            nonrobust
==============================================================================
                 coef    std err          t      P>|t|      [95.0% Conf. Int.]
------------------------------------------------------------------------------
Intercept     224.5840    520.609      0.431      0.669      -841.836  1291.004
ind_var_d      -1.1946      3.085     -0.387      0.702        -7.515     5.125
==============================================================================
Omnibus:                        0.043   Durbin-Watson:                   2.057
Prob(Omnibus):                  0.979   Jarque-Bera (JB):                0.058
Skew:                          -0.017   Prob(JB):                        0.971
Kurtosis:                       2.787   Cond. No.                     1.14e+03
==============================================================================
```

It's good to start our testing with a solid qualitative check to make sure we're starting from ground zero. Here you can see that Prob(F-statistic) is > .05. This should be interpreted to mean that we don't have enough evidence to conclude that any of our current beta coefficients are not zero. Said another way, we don't have a statistically valid model yet. Now to be fair, .05 is fairly arbitrary but it's a good rule of thumb. By the time we're done here, this number will be much smaller than .05 so it's a great baseline expectation.

Now let's code up our first expectation, that the Prob(F-statistic) is less than .05. Let's rewrite this test to no longer fail by default like so:

```
def vanilla_model_test():
  df = pandas.read_csv('./generated_data.csv')
  model_fit = sm.ols('dependent_var ~ ind_var_d', data=df).fit()
  print model_fit.summary()
  assert model_fit.f_pvalue <= 0.05, "Prob(F-statistic) should be
small enough to reject the null hypothesis."
```

Each of our variables should be assumed to contribute differing magnitudes to the final dependent variable we're trying to predict (or they can contribute nothing). In this case, ind_var_d contributes very little, if not nothing. So next I try to make this pass by trying one of the other independent variables in the data:

```
def vanilla_model_test():
  df = pandas.read_csv('./generated_data.csv')
  model_fit = sm.ols('dependent_var ~ ind_var_a', data=df).fit()
  print model_fit.summary()
  assert model_fit.f_pvalue <= 0.05, "Prob(F-statistic) should be
small enough to reject the null hypothesis."
```

By switching to independent variable a, our p-value for F-statistic goes below the number we want. Now let's see if we can get to a R_a^2 value that is greater than .95:

```
def vanilla_model_test():
  df = pandas.read_csv('./generated_data.csv')
  model_fit = sm.ols('dependent_var ~ ind_var_a', data=df).fit()
  print model_fit.summary()
  assert model_fit.f_pvalue <= 0.05, "Prob(F-statistic) should be
small enough to reject the null hypothesis."
  assert model_fit.rsquared_adj >= 0.95, "Model should explain 95%
of the variation in the sampled data or more."
```

This test fails with the following output:

```
                            OLS Regression Results
==============================================================================
Dep. Variable:          dependent_var   R-squared:                       0.182
Model:                            OLS   Adj. R-squared:                  0.152
Method:                 Least Squares   F-statistic:                     6.215
Date:                Thu, 19 Feb 2015   Prob (F-statistic):             0.0188
Time:                        21:16:15   Log-Likelihood:                 -219.98
No. Observations:                  30   AIC:                             444.0
Df Residuals:                      28   BIC:                             446.8
Df Model:                           1
Covariance Type:            nonrobust
==============================================================================
                 coef    std err          t      P>|t|      [95.0% Conf. Int.]
------------------------------------------------------------------------------
Intercept      33.4182     70.006      0.477      0.637     -109.982    176.819
ind_var_a       3.0475      1.222      2.493      0.019        0.544      5.551
==============================================================================
Omnibus:                        0.175   Durbin-Watson:                   1.811
Prob(Omnibus):                  0.916   Jarque-Bera (JB):                0.023
Skew:                          -0.053   Prob(JB):                        0.988
Kurtosis:                       2.915   Cond. No.                         57.3
==============================================================================
```

We can see why this failed. The R_a^2 value is only .152 so the current model only explains around 15% of the variation in our data. Also, until now, we've not really paid much attention to the output of our test results. Usually our tests failed in a very specific way and we had very little information to go by. Because we're testing the tuning of a pre-built algorithm to data, we have a rich set of summary information to guide us.

Let's include another variable and see how this performs. I make the following change to my model:

```
def vanilla_model_test():
  df = pandas.read_csv('./generated_data.csv')
  model_fit = sm.ols('dependent_var ~ ind_var_a + ind_var_b',
data=df).fit()
  print model_fit.summary()
  assert model_fit.f_pvalue <= 0.05, "Prob(F-statistic) should be
small enough to reject the null hypothesis."
  assert model_fit.rsquared_adj >= 0.95, "Model should explain 95%
of the variation in the sampled data or more."
```

Including the independent variable b causes our R_a^2 to jump to .804! Now we should also check the t-statistics for our variables just to make sure our initial variable is still needed. Looking at our new output one more time, we see the following:

```
                          OLS Regression Results
==============================================================================
Dep. Variable:         dependent_var   R-squared:                       0.818
Model:                           OLS   Adj. R-squared:                  0.804
Method:                Least Squares   F-statistic:                     60.62
Date:               Thu, 19 Feb 2015   Prob (F-statistic):           1.04e-10
Time:                       21:19:56   Log-Likelihood:                -197.44
No. Observations:                 30   AIC:                             400.9
Df Residuals:                     27   BIC:                             405.1
Df Model:                          2
Covariance Type:            nonrobust
==============================================================================
                 coef    std err          t      P>|t|      [95.0% Conf. Int.]
------------------------------------------------------------------------------
Intercept      94.5490     34.216      2.763      0.010      24.344     164.754
ind_var_a       2.7750      0.588      4.720      0.000       1.569       3.981
ind_var_b     115.1101     11.853      9.712      0.000      90.791     139.430
==============================================================================
Omnibus:                        0.248   Durbin-Watson:                   2.031
Prob(Omnibus):                  0.883   Jarque-Bera (JB):                0.442
Skew:                          -0.101   Prob(JB):                        0.802
Kurtosis:                       2.441   Cond. No.                         58.5
==============================================================================
```

So the p-value of the t-statistics for each variable are much less than 0.05. As a result, we should elect to keep the variables we have so far and add a new one. Let's try the next one ind_var_c:

```
def vanilla_model_test():
  df = pandas.read_csv('./generated_data.csv')
  model_fit = sm.ols('dependent_var ~ ind_var_a + ind_var_b +
ind_var_c', data=df).fit()
  print model_fit.summary()
  assert model_fit.f_pvalue <= 0.05, "Prob(F-statistic) should be
small enough to reject the null hypothesis."
  assert model_fit.rsquared_adj >= 0.95, "Model should explain 95%
of the variation in the sampled data or more."
```

This is an interesting one. Our R_a^2 value goes up a couple percentage points and the p-value for the new variable is 0.045. It's technically below our default cut-off of 0.05 but close enough to it we should keep a watch on this variable as we add new ones.

Let's keep going and add the independent variable d to see something different happen:

```
def vanilla_model_test():
  df = pandas.read_csv('./generated_data.csv')
  model_fit = sm.ols('dependent_var ~ ind_var_a + ind_var_b +
ind_var_c + ind_var_d', data=df).fit()
  print model_fit.summary()
  assert model_fit.f_pvalue <= 0.05, "Prob(F-statistic) should be
small enough to reject the null hypothesis."
  assert model_fit.rsquared_adj >= 0.95, "Model should explain 95%
of the variation in the sampled data or more."
```

The output is a spectacular case of what a no good variable looks like once added to our model:

```
                          OLS Regression Results
==============================================================================
Dep. Variable:          dependent_var   R-squared:                       0.845
Model:                            OLS   Adj. R-squared:                  0.820
Method:                 Least Squares   F-statistic:                     34.12
Date:                Thu, 19 Feb 2015   Prob (F-statistic):           8.64e-10
Time:                        21:33:11   Log-Likelihood:                -195.00
No. Observations:                  30   AIC:                             400.0
Df Residuals:                      25   BIC:                             407.0
Df Model:                           4
Covariance Type:            nonrobust
==============================================================================
                 coef    std err          t      P>|t|      [95.0% Conf. Int.]
------------------------------------------------------------------------------
Intercept     286.7307    225.631      1.271      0.216    -177.965     751.427
ind_var_a       2.5552      0.574      4.453      0.000       1.373       3.737
ind_var_b     112.2556     11.438      9.814      0.000      88.698     135.813
ind_var_c      -6.4966      3.134     -2.073      0.049     -12.951      -0.042
ind_var_d      -0.4223      1.293     -0.327      0.747      -3.085       2.240
==============================================================================
Omnibus:                        0.100   Durbin-Watson:                   2.208
Prob(Omnibus):                  0.951   Jarque-Bera (JB):                0.030
Skew:                           0.028   Prob(JB):                        0.985
Kurtosis:                       2.856   Cond. No.                     1.19e+03
==============================================================================
```

Let's go through the stats we've been watching. First our R_a^2 has stayed in almost exactly the same place and actually fell just slightly. This is also a great concrete reason why we should always use the R_a^2 value instead of the standard R^2 value. The standard value stayed the same but the adjusted value is penalized for having more variables in the model. As a result, since there was no added value but there was extra complexity, this score actually fell.

Next let's turn our attention to the p-values of our t-statistics. Notice every value is below 0.05 (independent variable c just barely), but independent variable d is *way* above it at 0.747.

These are signs that this variable hurts our model and we should exclude it. Next let's replace it with independent variable e and see what happens. I change the test to this:

```
def vanilla_model_test():
  df = pandas.read_csv('./generated_data.csv')
  model_fit = sm.ols('dependent_var ~ ind_var_a + ind_var_b +
ind_var_c + ind_var_e', data=df).fit()
```

```
print model_fit.summary()
    assert model_fit.f_pvalue <= 0.05, "Prob(F-statistic) should be
small enough to reject the null hypothesis."
    assert model_fit.rsquared_adj >= 0.95, "Model should explain 95%
of the variation in the sampled data or more."
```

This is another interesting case. My R_a^2 value goes up slightly to 0.836 but the new variable has a rather high p-value. It also has lowered the p-value for independent variable c. For now, let's keep this in the model since it increased the R_a^2 and see where else we can get to.

Next let's continue along by adding in independent variable f. The code is the same as you've seen at this point. The results are similar to when we added independent variable d. The R_a^2 value drops slightly and the p-value for the new variable is ridiculously high at 0.866. Again, we drop the bad variable and try the next one: independent variable g. Same story as before.

Last but not least, we try independent variable h but run into similar results. At this point, we've got a fairly solid model with the following code:

```
def vanilla_model_test():
    df = pandas.read_csv('./generated_data.csv')
    model_fit = sm.ols('dependent_var ~ ind_var_a + ind_var_b +
ind_var_c + ind_var_e', data=df).fit()
    print model_fit.summary()
    assert model_fit.f_pvalue <= 0.05, "Prob(F-statistic) should be
small enough to reject the null hypothesis."
    assert model_fit.rsquared_adj >= 0.95, "Model should explain 95%
of the variation in the sampled data or more."
```

Now we could just stop here and say that this is good enough. Seeing as how I generated the model though, I know we can still move this quite a bit. Next we can explore some interaction effects between our variables. For our first interaction, let's try adding variable a and b interacting. This is how we can represent this in our model:

```
def vanilla_model_test():
    df = pandas.read_csv('./generated_data.csv')
    model_fit = sm.ols('dependent_var ~ ind_var_a + ind_var_b +
ind_var_c + ind_var_e + ind_var_a * ind_var_b', data=df).fit()
    print model_fit.summary()
    assert model_fit.f_pvalue <= 0.05, "Prob(F-statistic) should be
small enough to reject the null hypothesis."
    assert model_fit.rsquared_adj >= 0.95, "Model should explain 95%
of the variation in the sampled data or more."
```

It's pretty straightforward. Having said that, this modification doesn't buy us anything in our model. As a matter of fact, not only does it not do anything, but it also lowers the predictive ability of some of our other variables. So let's throw that term out.

Next let's try modeling an interaction effect between independent variables b and c:

```
.
-----------------------------------------------------------------
Ran 1 test in 0.414s

OK
```

Bingo! Let's force a failure in the test just so we can see the summary:

```
                          OLS Regression Results
==============================================================================
Dep. Variable:          dependent_var   R-squared:                     0.987
Model:                           OLS    Adj. R-squared:                0.984
Method:                Least Squares    F-statistic:                   356.7
Date:               Thu, 19 Feb 2015    Prob (F-statistic):         1.07e-21
Time:                       22:02:03    Log-Likelihood:              -158.16
No. Observations:                 30    AIC:                           328.3
Df Residuals:                     24    BIC:                           336.7
Df Model:                          5
Covariance Type:           nonrobust
==============================================================================
                       coef    std err          t      P>|t|      [95.0% Conf. Int.]
------------------------------------------------------------------------------
Intercept           25.6266     24.999      1.025      0.316     -25.968     77.221
ind_var_a            2.7083      0.171     15.820      0.000       2.355      3.062
ind_var_b           -1.5527      8.798     -0.176      0.861     -19.712     16.606
ind_var_c           -0.3917      1.036     -0.378      0.709      -2.529      1.746
ind_var_e           -0.2006      0.032     -6.231      0.000      -0.267     -0.134
ind_var_b:ind_var_c  5.6450      0.371     15.225      0.000       4.880      6.410
==============================================================================
Omnibus:                       0.697    Durbin-Watson:                 2.070
Prob(Omnibus):                 0.706    Jarque-Bera (JB):              0.584
Skew:                         -0.318    Prob(JB):                      0.747
Kurtosis:                      2.750    Cond. No.                    1.48e+03
==============================================================================
```

We were able to find an R_a^2 value of 0.984. Also, notice how our p-value for independent variables b and c skyrocketed? That's fine, we'll still keep them in since we are modeling their interaction effects. In fact, if we tried to remove the independent variables and left the interaction effect in, we'd see that the model would manually add the independent variables back for us.

Cross-validating our model

Now before we cheat and look at our answer key, let's see how well this solution does at predicting data it hasn't seen. To do this, I write the following fairly large test:

```
def final_model_cross_validation_test():
  df = pandas.read_csv('./generated_data.csv')
  df['predicted_dependent_var'] = 25.6266 \
                            + 2.7083*df['ind_var_a'] \
                            - 1.5527*df['ind_var_b'] \
                            - 0.3917*df['ind_var_c'] \
                            - 0.2006*df['ind_var_e'] \
                            + 5.6450*df['ind_var_b'] * df['ind_
var_c']
  df['diff'] = (df['dependent_var'] -
df['predicted_dependent_var']).abs()
  print df['diff']
  print '==========='
  cv_df = pandas.read_csv('./generated_data_cv.csv')
  cv_df['predicted_dependent_var'] = 25.6266 \
                            + 2.7083*cv_df['ind_var_a'] \
                            - 1.5527*cv_df['ind_var_b'] \
                            - 0.3917*cv_df['ind_var_c'] \
                            - 0.2006*cv_df['ind_var_e'] \
                            + 5.6450*cv_df['ind_var_b'] * cv_
df['ind_var_c']
  cv_df['diff'] = (cv_df['dependent_var'] -
cv_df['predicted_dependent_var']).abs()
  print cv_df['diff']
  print cv_df['diff'].sum()/df['diff'].sum()

  assert cv_df['diff'].sum()/df['diff'].sum() - 1 <= .05,
  "Cross-validated data should have roughly the same error as
  original model."
```

What this is doing is taking the parameters for the model we discovered, plugging in the various variables in our model, and predicting what our dependent variable's value should be. For each prediction, we find the absolute value of the difference and then compare the sum of the difference between both the model acting on our original data and the model acting on a fresh set of data generated with the same process.

Our test says that the errors have to be within 5% of those of the original model. When you run this test though, you will probably find that the errors on the fresh data are actually less than .05.

Generating data

Now that we've gone through the process of searching for the right model, let's talk about what the model's true parameters were and how they line up with the parameters our regression generated.

This is the code that was used to generate the data:

```python
import numpy as np

variable_a = np.random.uniform(-100, 100, 30)
variable_b = np.random.uniform(-5, 5, 30)
variable_c = np.random.uniform(0, 37, 30)
variable_d = np.random.uniform(121, 213, 30)
variable_e = np.random.uniform(-1000, 100, 30)
variable_f = np.random.uniform(-100, 100, 30)
variable_g = np.random.uniform(-25, 75, 30)
variable_h = np.random.uniform(1, 27, 30)

independent_variables = zip(variable_a, variable_b, variable_c,
variable_d, variable_e, variable_f, variable_g, variable_h)
dependent_variables = [3*x[0] - 2*x[1] - .25*x[4] + 5.75*x[1]*x[2]
+ np.random.normal(0, 50) for x in  independent_variables]

full_dataset = [x[0] + (x[1],) for x in zip(independent_variables,
dependent_variables)]

import csv
with open('generated_data.csv', 'wb') as f:
    writer = csv.writer(f)
    writer.writerow(['ind_var_a', 'ind_var_b', 'ind_var_c',
'ind_var_d', 'ind_var_e', 'ind_var_f', 'ind_var_g', 'ind_var_h',
'dependent_var'])
    writer.writerows(full_dataset)
```

First let's talk about the formula used to create the dependent variable on line 13. Restated, it basically says:

$$y = 3x_a - 2x_b - .25x_e + 5.75x_b x_c + N(0,50)$$

So that's what we should have ended up with. What we did end up with was:

$$2.7083x_a - 1.5527x_b - 0.3917x_c - 0.2006x_e + 5.645x_bx_c + 25.6266$$

Our terms are fairly close. We had the extra independent variable c term show up in our computed solution and a constant tacked onto the end. If you're wondering where the constant came from, look again at the original equation. The constant is the product of the normal random variable we've tacked onto the end.

You can use this technique to continue exploring regression as well as to build datasets with which to test stepwise regression algorithms or whatever else you can think of. By generating the data, it gives you an opportunity to truly dig into what is happening in your models. It can also help you practice building models, since you can check your answer after the fact.

Summary

In this chapter, we stepped through what it takes to drive building a multiple regression model using the same unit test techniques we've been using to develop code.

In the next chapter, we will continue with exploring regression but will move on to **logistic regression**. Rather than predicting values, we'll use logistic regression to classify data into one group or another.

5
Making Decisions Black and White with Logistic Regression

In the last chapter, we used regression to predict values over a continuous range. In this chapter, we will explore the tuning of a regression model that predicts a binary classification. You are probably already pretty familiar with this method, so we'll spend just time introducing the aspects that we'll be leveraging.

The most important thing about logistic regression is that its form is very different from linear regression. Likewise, interpreting the results is also different and quite confusing. A standard N-variable logistic regression model has the following form:

$$E\left(y\right) = \frac{e^{\beta_0 + \beta_1 x_1 + \beta_2 x_2 + \cdots + \beta_n x_n}}{1 + e^{\beta_0 + \beta_1 x_1 + \beta_2 x_2 + \cdots + \beta_n x_n}}$$

While in linear regression, the beta coefficient represents the change for every unit of change in the associated x variable. In logistic regression, the betas represent the change in log-odds for every unit's increase in the associated x variable. As a result of this very difference in the model, the way in which we generate data will need to be changed a bit as well.

In this chapter, we will be applying test-driven techniques to develop a logistic regression model that can be used for classifying data. Most importantly, we'll learn how to quantify the model quality in such a way that we can automate our determination of whether or not each iteration of our model is better than before.

Generating logistic data

A critical aspect of test driving our process is being in control. In the last chapter, we fitted a model to a pregenerated set of test data, and tried to guess what the beta coefficients were. In this chapter, we'll start generating a very simple dataset, and then we'll compute the estimates for the coefficients that we'll use. This will help us understand how this all comes together so that we can be sure that we're driving our code in the right direction.

Here is how we can generate some simple data:

```
import pandas
import statsmodels.formula.api as smf
import numpy as np

observation_count = 1000
intercept = -1.6
beta1 = 0.03
x = np.random.uniform(0, 100, size=observation_count)
x_prime = [np.exp(intercept + beta1 * x_i) / (1 + np.exp(intercept +
beta1 * x_i)) for x_i in x]
y = [np.random.binomial(1, x_prime_i, size=1)[0] for x_prime_i in x_
prime]
df = pandas.DataFrame({'x':x, 'y':y})
```

We will sample the data from a binomial distribution, because its values stick between zero and one, and the result will hover around the value that is fed into it, but with some noise. We can check that this is correct by fitting this model. We will know whether it was successful because the predicted beta coefficients should be very close to the betas that we've specified. Here is how we fit this model using statsmodels in Python:

```
model = smf.logit('y ~ x', df)
fit = model.fit()
fit.summary()
```

Notice that in the code where the data is generated, the `intercept` is set to `-1.6`, and `beta1` is set to `0.03`. These are the values that we're looking for our model to predict. The summary will look something like the following:

Logit Regression Results			
Dep. Variable:	y	**No. Observations:**	1000
Model:	Logit	**Df Residuals:**	998
Method:	MLE	**Df Model:**	1
Date:	Sun, 01 Mar 2015	**Pseudo R-squ.:**	0.1476
Time:	16:02:11	**Log-Likelihood:**	-589.61
converged:	True	**LL-Null:**	-691.69
		LLR p-value:	2.598e-46

	coef	**std err**	**z**	**P>|z|**	**[95.0% Conf. Int.]**
Intercept	-1.8773	0.156	-12.055	0.000	-2.182 -1.572
x	0.0349	0.003	12.897	0.000	0.030 0.040

Our model acknowledges that most likely intercept is -1.8773, and the most likely value of x (known as beta1 in our data generation code) is 0.0349. These are both pretty close to the actual values we've used to generate the data. On top of this, both intercept and beta coefficient are contained within the 95 percent confidence interval for each parameter. Next, let's review some indicators of the model quality.

One method of confirming that a model has some sort of predictive power is by noting the Likelihood Ratio p-value. For the purposes of this book, we typically define significance as a p-value of less than 0.05. We can find the value we're after in the previous summary named LLR p-value. It's almost zero, so we can have a pretty high confidence that at least one of our parameters is non-zero, and thus we have an adequate model.

Measuring model accuracy

So, we know how to create a model that is "adequate", but what does this really mean? How can we differentiate whether one "adequate" model is better than another? A common approach is to compare the ROC curves. This one is generated from the simple model that we just created:

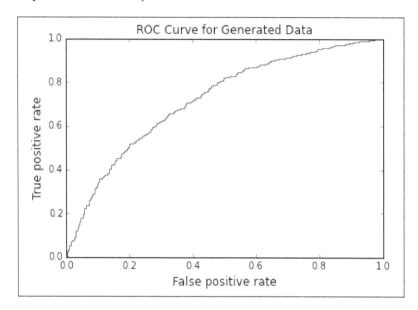

You're probably familiar with ROC curves. They show us what kind of true positive rate we can achieve by allowing a given error rate in terms of false positives. The basic take away is that we want the curve to get as close to the upper left corner as possible. In case you haven't used these visualizations before, the reason for this is that the more the line is pulled up and to the left, the fewer false positives we get for every true positive. It maps very much to the concept of an error rate.

We have a visualization, which is great, but we can't automatically test it. We need to find some way to quantify this phenomenon. There is a simple, pretty straightforward way. It's called an **Area Under Curve score (AUC score)**.

AUC works by finding the area under our previous ROC curve. You can see that if the lines were pulled all the way up, and were to the left under the curve, then it would just be the full area of the square containing the graph or 1.0. If the curve was just a straight diagonal line from the lower-left to upper-right part, then it would indicate random performance. The area under that curve would be 0.5. Typically, we'll see the values situated somewhere between these two values.

Why can't it be less than 0.5? Well, in this case, we can get a score above 0.5 by doing the opposite of what the model says. After all, if we're able to make good decisions by consistently doing the opposite of the model's recommendations, then it's actually very useful. In practice, we'd then just invert the model's results, and we'd be back to an **AUC** score between 0.5 and 1.0.

The **AUC** score for the previous graph is around 0.722. If you're wondering how to reproduce this work, here is the code that I used to create the chart and the calculation:

```
import sklearn.metrics
import matplotlib.pyplot as plt

roc_data = sklearn.metrics.roc_curve(df['y'], fit.predict(df))
plt..title("ROC Curve for Generated Data")
plt.xlabel("False positive rate",fontsize=12)
plt.ylabel("True positive rate",fontsize=12)
plt.plot(roc_data[0], roc_data[1])
print "AUC: {0}".format(sklearn.metrics.auc(roc_data[0], roc_data[1]))
plt.show()
```

Generating a more complex example

Up until now, we've been looking at a very simple set of data. Next, we'll be generating a much more complicated example. To model it, we'll be applying the techniques from the last chapter to build a solid model using TDD.

Unlike the last time, let's build the data generation code first, and use it so that it can help us understand our model building process more deeply. Here is the data generator that we'll use for the remainder of this chapter:

```
import pandas
import statsmodels.formula.api as smf
import numpy as np

def generate_data():
    observation_count = 1000
    intercept = -1.6
    beta1 = -0.03
    beta2 = 0.1
    beta3 = -0.15
    variable_a = np.random.uniform(0, 100, size=observation_count)
    variable_b = np.random.uniform(50, 75, size=observation_count)
    variable_c = np.random.uniform(3, 10, size=observation_count)
```

```
      variable_d = np.random.uniform(3, 10, size=observation_count)
      variable_e = np.random.uniform(11, 87, size=observation_count)
      x = zip(variable_a, variable_b, variable_c, variable_d,
variable_e)
      x_prime = [np.exp(intercept + beta1 * x_i[0] + beta2 * x_i[1] +
beta3 * x_i[2]) / (1 + np.exp(intercept + beta1 * x_i[0] + beta2 *
x_i[1] + beta3 * x_i[2])) for x_i in x]
      y = [np.random.binomial(1, x_prime_i, size=1)[0] for x_prime_i in
x_prime]
      df = pandas.DataFrame({
          'variable_a': variable_a,
          'variable_b': variable_b,
          'variable_c': variable_c,
          'variable_d': variable_d,
          'variable_e': variable_e,
          'y':y})
      return df


generate_data().to_csv('generated_logistic_data.csv')
```

This script establishes the values of `intercept`, `beta1`, `beta2`, and `beta3`. Then it generates random data for five variables. Next, it uses three of these variables to create a variable that we imagine as the classifications for the data. Again, we note that because we are generating data for logistic regression, the creation of our *y* variable is not as straightforward as it was in our linear regression data.

From here, we'll stuff all of the generated data into a `DataFrame`, return it, and then write it in a file on disk.

For the remaining part of the chapter, we'll play ignorant and explore, starting off with a terrible model. We'll quantify it and iterate to improve it.

Test driving our model

To start with now, we must create the framework for scoring our model in a test. It will look like the following:

```
import pandas
import sklearn.metrics
import statsmodels.formula.api as smf
import numpy as np

def logistic_regression_test():
    df = pandas.DataFrame.from_csv('./generated_logistic_data.csv')
    generated_model = smf.logit('y ~ variable_d', df)
```

```
    generated_fit = generated_model.fit()
    roc_data = sklearn.metrics.roc_curve(df['y'], generated_fit.
predict(df))
    auc = sklearn.metrics.auc(roc_data[0], roc_data[1])
    print generated_fit.summary()
    print "AUC score: {0}".format(auc)
    assert auc > .6, 'AUC should be significantly above random'
```

The previous code also includes a first stab at a model. Because we generated the data, we know that `variable_d` is completely unhelpful, but it makes this a bit more of an interesting exploration.

When we run the previous code, the test fails, as expected. I have the test set up to give the full statistical summary, as well as the AUC score on the test failure to help us debug. Then, the following is displayed:

```
F
==================================================================
FAIL: logistic_regression_tests.logistic_regression_test
------------------------------------------------------------------
Traceback (most recent call last):
  File "/Library/Python/2.7/site-packages/nose-1.3.0-py2.7.egg/nose/ca
se.py", line 197, in runTest
    self.test(*self.arg)
  File "/Users/justin/Documents/Code/Machine-Learning-Test-by-Test/Cha
pter 5/logistic_regression_tests.py", line 13, in logistic_regression_
test
    assert auc > .6, 'AUC should be significantly above random'
AssertionError: AUC should be significantly above random
-------------------- >> begin captured stdout << ----------------------
Optimization terminated successfully.
         Current function value: 0.426086
         Iterations 6
AUC score: 0.510791645978

-------------------- >> end captured stdout << ----------------------


------------------------------------------------------------------
Ran 1 test in 0.527s

FAILED (failures=1)
```

Now we see that the AUC score is only .51. We can look at the summary that is displayed:

```
                     Logit Regression Results
==============================================================================
Dep. Variable:                    y   No. Observations:             1000
Model:                        Logit   Df Residuals:                  998
Method:                         MLE   Df Model:                        1
Date:             Sun, 01 Mar 2015   Pseudo R-squ.:             0.0001789
Time:                      21:16:05   Log-Likelihood:            -426.09
converged:                     True   LL-Null:                   -426.16
                                      LLR p-value:                0.6962
==============================================================================
                 coef    std err          z      P>|z|      [95.0% Conf. Int.]
------------------------------------------------------------------------------
Intercept      1.8273      0.292      6.258      0.000       1.255      2.400
variable_d    -0.0167      0.043     -0.390      0.696      -0.101      0.067
==============================================================================
```

Since we have the **AUC** score, we already know that this model isn't great, but let's take a look at it and see how its numbers line up with our expectations.

We can see that the **Likelihood Ratio p-value** is insanely high at 0.69, when we generally want it lower than 0.05. The p-value on `variable_d` is also very high at 0.696. In general, all of these numbers agree that the model so far is terrible. For the sake of space, we won't look at the full statistical summary again until something changes dramatically.

Next, let's swap out `variable_d` for `variable_e` and see how it performs. The test that we'll run looks like the following:

```
def logistic_regression_test():
  df = pandas.DataFrame.from_csv('./generated_logistic_data.csv')

  generated_model = smf.logit('y ~ variable_e', df)
  generated_fit = generated_model.fit()
  roc_data = sklearn.metrics.roc_curve(df['y'], generated_fit.
predict(df))
  auc = sklearn.metrics.auc(roc_data[0], roc_data[1])
  print generated_fit.summary()
  print "AUC score: {0}".format(auc)
  assert auc > .6, 'AUC should be significantly above random'
```

The only line that we really need to change is the one where we specify the model with `'y ~ variable_e'`. After running with this model, all of the stats become roughly the same. The new **AUC** is 0.51.

Neither of these variables seem helpful. Let's try `variable_c` next. We'll now change to the following model:

```
generated_model = smf.logit('y ~ variable_c', df)
```

Now, this causes something interesting. The Likelihood Ratio p-value is suddenly great at 0.01! This is a great time to point out how a great test of model adequacy does *not* imply a great model fit. The AUC score is 0.566. It is definitely better, but it is not even at our first milestone. Next, let's add one of the other variables to our model, as follows:

```
generated_model = smf.logit('y ~ variable_b + variable_c', df)
```

Adding `variable_b` allows us a test that passes. Let's up our milestone to 0.70, and see where we've reached:

```
def logistic_regression_test():
    df = pandas.DataFrame.from_csv('./generated_logistic_data.csv')

    generated_model = smf.logit('y ~ variable_b + variable_c', df)
    generated_fit = generated_model.fit()
    roc_data = sklearn.metrics.roc_curve(df['y'], generated_fit.
predict(df))
    auc = sklearn.metrics.auc(roc_data[0], roc_data[1])
    print generated_fit.summary()
    print "AUC score: {0}".format(auc)
    assert auc > .7, 'AUC should be significantly above random'
```

Our test fails again. Now that we've passed our first milestone, let's again check with the statistical summary:

```
                           Logit Regression Results
==============================================================================
Dep. Variable:                      y   No. Observations:                 1000
Model:                          Logit   Df Residuals:                      997
Method:                           MLE   Df Model:                            2
Date:                Sun, 01 Mar 2015   Pseudo R-squ.:                  0.06133
Time:                        21:36:58   Log-Likelihood:                 -400.03
converged:                       True   LL-Null:                        -426.16
                                        LLR p-value:                  4.464e-12
==============================================================================
                 coef    std err          z      P>|z|      [95.0% Conf. Int.]
------------------------------------------------------------------------------
Intercept      -2.7924      0.852     -3.278      0.001       -4.462     -1.123
variable_b      0.0878      0.014      6.445      0.000        0.061      0.114
variable_c     -0.1242      0.045     -2.783      0.005       -0.212     -0.037
==============================================================================
AUC score: 0.678741000497
```

After hitting our first milestone, it looks like we've landed on an AUC of 0.679. We still have a Likelihood Ration p-value that is quite tiny (practically zero at this point). Also, notice that the p-value of each parameter of the model is indeed below 0.05. Your answers will vary, but they should be quite close to this...

We have one more variable that we can try to include in our `variable_a` model. We'll update our model as follows:

```
generated_model = smf.logit('y ~ variable_a + variable_b +
variable_c', df)
```

Finally, our test passes, which indicates that we've passed our next milestone. Upping the target **AUC** to 0.8 still results in a test that passes. Moving it up to 0.9 causes the test to break. Again, you may notice slightly different results, but they should be fairly close. We should see a summary like the following:

```
                        Logit Regression Results
==============================================================================
Dep. Variable:                      y   No. Observations:                 1000
Model:                          Logit   Df Residuals:                      996
Method:                           MLE   Df Model:                            3
Date:                Sun, 01 Mar 2015   Pseudo R-squ.:                  0.2088
Time:                        21:44:45   Log-Likelihood:                 -337.19
converged:                       True   LL-Null:                        -426.16
                                        LLR p-value:                  2.458e-38
==============================================================================
                 coef    std err          z      P>|z|      [95.0% Conf. Int.]
------------------------------------------------------------------------------
Intercept      -0.9958      0.932     -1.068      0.286      -2.823      0.832
variable_a     -0.0392      0.004     -9.828      0.000      -0.047     -0.031
variable_b      0.0996      0.015      6.677      0.000       0.070      0.129
variable_c     -0.1487      0.049     -3.048      0.002      -0.244     -0.053
==============================================================================
AUC score: 0.813842167329
```

We still have a bit of a journey to get to an **AUC** of 0.9, but this model is definitely better than random guessing. Every parameter is pretty solid. The intercept is the only parameter whose p-value is not less than 0.05, but it's automatically included, so it's an exception to the rule.

Try adding in one of the variables that we already discarded to see if it gets us farther along.

You've probably noticed that you can squeeze out a tiny bit more **AUC**, but only to a point where it was probably negligible. By knowing what the true model is, we can definitely say that adding the other variables is negligible.

Make sure to set the test back to a target **AUC** of 0.8 for your test to pass, and we're done here.

In the end, our model predicted the following:

- Intercept- Predicted -0.9958 actually -1.6
- Beta1- Predicted -0.0392 actually -0.03
- Beta2- Predicted 0.0996 actually 0.1
- Beta3- Predicted -0.1487 actually -0.15

The intercept is a bit off, but all in all our model does a pretty great job of reproducing the parameters that we've used to generate our data.

Summary

In this chapter, we reviewed logistic regression and different measures of quality. We figured out how to quantify the typically qualitative measures of quality, and then we used them to drive us through a model building process test first.

In the next chapter, we'll continue exploring classification by looking at one of the most straightforward techniques that we'll learn about the Naïve Bayes classification.

6
You're So Naïve, Bayes

We've all seen examples of using Naïve Bayes classifiers in a way of classifying text. The applications include spam detection, sentiment analysis, and more. In this chapter, we're going to take a road that is less traveled. We will build a Naïve Bayes classifier that can take in continuous inputs and classify them. Specifically, we'll build a Gaussian Naïve Bayes classifier to classify which state a person is from, which will be based on the person's height, weight, and BMI.

This chapter will work a bit differently from the previous ones. Here, we'll develop an N-class Gaussian Naïve Bayes classifier to fit our use case (the data at hand). In the next chapter, we'll pull in some of this data to train with, and then we'll analyze the quality of our model to see how we did it. In the previous chapters, we used generated data so that we could make sure that the classifiers built by us were operating according to their assumptions. In this chapter, we'll spend most of our time just building the classifier. Once we get to the next chapter, we'll test it with some fake data just to make sure that it meets our expectations. After which, we'll switch to real data. At which point, it's anybody's guess how well we'll do.

The development of this classifier takes some interesting turns from a TDD perspective. Since we won't be going through all of the standard model validation steps, the journey should be even more rewarding as a result.

Gaussian classification by hand

Since the Gaussian Naïve Bayes classifier is less common, let's discuss it a bit more before diving in. The Gaussian Naïve Bayes algorithm works by taking in values that are continuous, and by assuming that they are all independent and that each variable follows a Gaussian (or Normal) distribution. It may not be obvious how a probability follows from this, so let's look at a concrete example.

Let's say that I give you five weights from the female test subjects and five weights from the male test subjects. Next, I want to give you a weight from a test subject of an unknown gender, and have you guess whether it's a man or woman. Using a Gaussian classifier, we can approach this problem by first defining an underlying Gaussian model for both, female and male observations (two models in total). A Gaussian model is specified using a mean and variance. Let's step through this with some numbers.

Let's assume that the following data is provided:

- The weight of five random women is 157, 165, 133, 192, and 101 respectively
- The weight of five random men is 203, 237, 180, 156, and 308 respectively

The observation that we want to categorize is 182. We want to find $P(F|W)$ (probability of a female given a weight). The probability of observing a single data value from a normal distribution, given the mean and variance, is provided by the following equation:

$$P(D|\mu,\sigma) = \frac{1}{\sigma\sqrt{2\pi}} e^{-\frac{(D-\mu)^2}{2\sigma^2}}$$

Here, D is the data that we have observed. In order to utilize this to solve our problem, we first need to find the mean and variance of the women's data:

- Mean = 149.6
- Variance = 945.44

Now, for the male observations:

- Mean = 216.8
- Variance = 2793.36

Now, we can ask; what is the chance of observing this new weight assuming that the person is a woman, and we can also answer this question assuming that they are a man. If this is to be said in another way, then we have the following:

$$P(W|\mu_f,\sigma_f) = \frac{1}{\sqrt{2\pi * 945.44}} e^{-\frac{1}{2}*\frac{(182-149.6)^2}{945.44}} = 0.74\%$$

$$P\left(W \mid \mu_m, \sigma_m\right) = \frac{1}{\sqrt{2\pi * 2793.36}} e^{-\frac{1}{2} * \frac{(182-216.8)^2}{2793.36}} = 0.61\%$$

Just by seeing this, we now know our observation is that the person is more likely a woman, but this isn't the exact question that we want to answer. What we really need to know is that what is $P\left(\mu_f, \sigma_f \mid W\right)$ and $P\left(\mu_m, \sigma_m \mid W\right)$. Using Bayes Law, we have:

$$P\left(\mu_f, \sigma_f \mid W\right) = \frac{P\left(W \mid \mu_f, \sigma_f\right) P\left(\mu_f, \sigma_f\right)}{P\left(W \mid \mu_f, \sigma_f\right) P\left(\mu_f, \sigma_f\right) + P\left(W \mid \mu_m, \sigma_m\right) P\left(\mu_m, \sigma_m\right)}$$

The $P\left(\mu_m, \sigma_m\right)$ might seem complicated, but it's really just the probability of being a male, which is just 50%. We can plug in the values that we've calculated now, and see if our chances lean more towards the person being male or female.

$$P\left(\mu_f, \sigma_f \mid W\right) = \frac{0.0074 * 0.5}{0.0074 * 0.5 + 0.0061 * 0.5} = 54.8\%$$

It's definitely not a clear-cut case, but if our classifier had to make a decision, it would classify this person as a woman.

Beginning the development

We start with the standard simplistic tests that will serve to get the basic wiring up for our classifier. First, the test:

```
import NaiveBayes

def no_observations_test():
  classifier = NaiveBayes.Classifier()
  classification = classifier.classify(observation=23.2)
  assert classification is None, "Should not classify observations
without training examples."
```

And then the code:

```
class Classifier:
  def classify(self, observation):
    pass
```

As the next step to approach a solution, let's try the case where we've only observed the data from a single class:

```
def given_an_observation_for_a_single_class_test():
  classifier = NaiveBayes.Classifier()
  classifier.train(classification='a class', observation=0)
  classification = classifier.classify(observation=23.2)
  assert classification == 'a class', "Should always classify as given
class if there is only one."
```

A very simple solution is to just set a single classification that gets set every time we train something:

```
class Classifier:
  def __init__(self):
    self._classification = None
  def train(self, classification, observation):
    self._classification = classification
  def classify(self, observation):
    return self._classification
```

This works well enough for us at this point. Now, we need to figure out what our next test will be. Let's try generalizing in order to support two classes and one observation in a piece. The following is a way of writing a test for this:

```
def given_one_observation_for_two_classes_test():
  classifier = NaiveBayes.Classifier()
  classifier.train(classification='a class', observation=0)
  classifier.train(classification='b class', observation=100)
  classification = classifier.classify(observation=23.2)
  assert classification == 'a class', "Should classify as the nearest
class."
  classification = classifier.classify(observation=73.2)
  assert classification == 'b class', "Should classify as the nearest
class."
```

This has two asserts, because we want to be certain that we aren't just returning the last trained class as the classification (just as we were doing). Perhaps, you do know the code you would really like to write. We can do some refactoring here to make our test easier to pass. We'll apply the following refactoring, and make sure that our previously passing tests continue to pass:

```
class Classifier:
  def __init__(self):
    self._classifications = {}
  def train(self, classification, observation):
```

```
        self._classifications[classification] = observation
    def classify(self, observation):
        if len(self._classifications.keys()) == 0:
            return None
        else:
            closest_class = self._classifications.keys()[0]
            closest_observation = abs(observation - self._
classifications[closest_class])
            return closest_class
```

From here, there's only a small way to go to get our new test to pass. We just need to loop through all of the classifications, and find the nearest one to our observation:

```
class Classifier:
    def __init__(self):
        self._classifications = {}
    def train(self, classification, observation):
        self._classifications[classification] = observation
    def classify(self, observation):
        if len(self._classifications.keys()) == 0:
            return None
        else:
            closest_class = self._classifications.keys()[0]
            closest_observation = abs(observation - self._
classifications[closest_class])
            for the_class, trained_observation in self._classifications.
items():
                if abs(observation - trained_observation) < closest_
observation:
                    closest_class = the_class
                    closest_observation = abs(observation - self._
classifications[closest_class])
            return closest_class
```

Now this, of course, isn't exactly what we want to do, but it definitely gets us one step closer. The test case is the one that should still work as we continue to improve our classifier.

In this next test, we will start to get at the meat and potatoes as it were. We'll keep the two classes, but let's write a test that will flex the Gaussian model, which we want to underlie our classifier. In the last test, we looked at the simple distance of classifying our data, but in this test, we'll make one class have a very tight variance, and another one that's very wide. Here's an example of a test that captures this effect:

```
def given_multiple_observations_for_two_classes_test():
    classifier = NaiveBayes.Classifier()
```

```
classifier.train(classification='a class', observation=0.0)
classifier.train(classification='a class', observation=1.0)
classifier.train(classification='a class', observation=0.5)
classifier.train(classification='b class', observation=50)
classifier.train(classification='b class', observation=15)
classifier.train(classification='b class', observation=100)
classification = classifier.classify(observation=23.2)
assert classification == 'b class', "Should classify as the best fit
class."
classification = classifier.classify(observation=2.0)
assert classification == 'a class', "Should classify as the best fit
class."
```

This test fails! Now, think about how you plan to get the test to pass. Since we need to handle multiple observations, let's refactor to store our, so far, single values in arrays so that we can easily generalize to what our test will need. After the refactoring, you will be left with a class that resembles the following:

```
class Classifier:
  def __init__(self):
    self._classifications = {}
  def train(self, classification, observation):
    if not classification in self._classifications:
      self._classifications[classification] = []
    self._classifications[classification].append(observation)
  def classify(self, observation):
    if len(self._classifications.keys()) == 0:
      return None
    else:
      closest_class = self._classifications.keys()[0]
      closest_observation = abs(observation - self._
classifications[closest_class][0])
      for the_class, trained_observations in self._classifications.
items():
        if abs(observation - trained_observations[0]) < closest_
observation:
          closest_class = the_class
          closest_observation = abs(observation - self._
classifications[closest_class][0])
    return closest_class
```

It turns out this probably isn't the simplest way to do what we need. We'll talk about this after we can discuss the resulting code. This is the class that we get after we succeed:

```python
import numpy as np

class Classifier:
  def __init__(self):
    self._classifications = {}
  def train(self, classification, observation):
    if not classification in self._classifications:
      self._classifications[classification] = []
    self._classifications[classification].append(observation)
  def _probability_given_class(self, trained_observations,
observation):
    variance = np.var(trained_observations)
    mean = np.mean(trained_observations)
    return 1/np.sqrt(2*np.pi*variance) * np.exp(-0.5*((observation -
mean)**2)/variance)
  def _probability_of_class_given_observation(self, the_class, other_
classes, p_of_observation_given_class):
    return p_of_observation_given_class[the_class]/(p_of_observation_
given_class[the_class] + sum([p_of_observation_given_class[other_
class] for other_class in other_classes]))
  def classify(self, observation):
    if len(self._classifications.keys()) == 0:
      return None
    else:
      classes = set(self._classifications.keys())
      highest_probability = 0
      best_class = self._classifications.keys()[0]
      probability_of_observation_given_class={}
      for the_class, trained_observations in self._classifications.
items():
        probability_of_observation_given_class[the_class] = self._
probability_given_class(trained_observations, observation)
      for the_class in probability_of_observation_given_class:
        candidate_probability = self._probability_of_class_given_
observation(the_class, classes-set(the_class), probability_of_
observation_given_class)
        candidate_class = the_class
        if candidate_probability > highest_probability:
          highest_probability = candidate_probability
          best_class = candidate_class
      return best_class
```

A lot of things have changed — too much, really. Let's reflect and talk about why. The refactoring where we generalized a bit of the code was a smell. We didn't have a test that required us to assume more than two classes, but a test that found it easier to code for it. Also, notice that the whole probability function called `_probability_given_class` was included in this run too. We can somewhat fix this by doubling back and putting some tests on the probability function to make sure it's working.

We still have a failing test though. We were able to get the latest test to pass, but one of our previous tests started failing. The test that is failing is called `given_one_observation_for_two_classes_test` and it is failing due to the fact that the variance of a single number is zero.

So, while the test helped us get to where we are, it's not really much of a help. Let's change this test to return none if we have only one trained instance for any class. Due to this, I've changed the test to the following:

```
def given_one_observation_for_two_classes_test():
  classifier = NaiveBayes.Classifier()
  classifier.train(classification='a class', observation=0)
  classifier.train(classification='b class', observation=100)
  classification = classifier.classify(observation=23.2)
  assert classification is None, "Should not classify if there is only
one observation in any class."
  classification = classifier.classify(observation=73.2)
  assert classification is None, "Should not classify if there is only
one observation in any class"
```

And then change the classify function to have the following, if you're in the middle of the classification process:

```
def classify(self, observation):
  if len(self._classifications.keys()) == 0:
    return None
  else:
    classes = set(self._classifications.keys())
    highest_probability = 0
    best_class = self._classifications.keys()[0]
    probability_of_observation_given_class={}
    for the_class, trained_observations in self._classifications.
items():
      if len(trained_observations) <= 1:
        return None
      probability_of_observation_given_class[the_class] = self._
probability_given_class(trained_observations, observation)
      print probability_of_observation_given_class
```

```
        for the_class in probability_of_observation_given_class:
            candidate_probability = self._probability_of_class_given_
    observation(the_class, classes-set(the_class), probability_of_
    observation_given_class)
            candidate_class = the_class
            print candidate_probability
            if candidate_probability > highest_probability:
                highest_probability = candidate_probability
                best_class = candidate_class
        return best_class
```

This solves the test, but we have one other test that makes no sense now called `given_an_observation_for_a_single_class_test`.

We change that test to look like the following:

```
def given_an_observation_for_a_single_class_test():
    classifier = NaiveBayes.Classifier()
    classifier.train(classification='a class', observation=0)
    classification = classifier.classify(observation=23.2)
    assert classification is None, "Should not classify if there is only
one observation in any class."
```

Rerunning the tests shows that everything is passed. Phew! This was terrible, but also important to go through. In your own practice, look out for possible issues similar to this, and give them extra thought to untangle the issues.

As a result of this, let's take a step back and revert to where we were. How could we refactor into something that will prevent us from needing to generalize, able to handle many classes right off the bat. So let's back up a second and revisit where we were before things went bad:

```
class Classifier:
    def __init__(self):
        self._classifications = {}
    def train(self, classification, observation):
        if not classification in self._classifications:
            self._classifications[classification] = []
        self._classifications[classification].append(observation)
    def classify(self, observation):
        if len(self._classifications.keys()) == 0:
            return None
        else:
            closest_class = self._classifications.keys()[0]
            closest_observation = abs(observation - self._
classifications[closest_class][0])
```

```
        for the_class, trained_observations in self._classifications.
items():
            if abs(observation - trained_observations[0]) < closest_
observation:
              closest_class = the_class
              closest_observation = abs(observation - self._
classifications[closest_class][0])
        return closest_class
```

The kind of refactoring that we can do is to stop using a dictionary for the data. Using a dictionary seems to be what had led us down a bad road earlier. Its ability to deal with as many classifications as we can throw at it makes us have to start dealing with more than two classifications. We don't want to do this right now. We have plenty of other problems to solve.

The following is the code after the refactoring:

```
class Classifier:
  def __init__(self):
    self._classification_a_label = None
    self._classification_a = None
    self._classification_b_label = None
    self._classification_b = None

  def train(self, classification, observation):
    if classification == self._classification_a_label:
      self._classification_a = observation
    elif classification == self._classification_b_label:
      self._classification_b = observation
    elif self._classification_a is None:
      self._classification_a_label = classification
      self._classification_a = observation
    elif self._classification_b is None:
      self._classification_b_label = classification
      self._classification_b = observation

  def classify(self, observation):
    if self._classification_a_label is None and self._
classification_b_label is None:
      return None
    elif self._classification_b_label is None:
      return self._classification_a_label
    else:
      closest_class = self._classification_a_label
```

```
        closest_observation = abs(observation - self._classification_a)
        if abs(observation - self._classification_b) < closest_
observation:
            closest_class = self._classification_b_label
        return closest_class
```

Once we finish the refactoring, we can run all of our tests and make sure they still pass. They do.

Our next step is to get the code to support multiple observations in either of the classes. In order to do this, we can refactor the code. You can see the small amount of changes necessary to position our code for more than one observation per class:

```
class Classifier:
  def __init__(self):
    self._classification_a_label = None
    self._classification_a = None
    self._classification_b_label = None
    self._classification_b = None

  def train(self, classification, observation):
    if classification == self._classification_a_label:
      self._classification_a.append(observation)
    elif classification == self._classification_b_label:
      self._classification_b.append(observation)
    elif self._classification_a is None:
      self._classification_a_label = classification
      self._classification_a = [observation]
    elif self._classification_b is None:
      self._classification_b_label = classification
      self._classification_b = [observation]

  def classify(self, observation):
    if self._classification_a_label is None and self._
classification_b_label is None:
      return None
    elif self._classification_b_label is None:
      return self._classification_a_label
    else:
      closest_class = self._classification_a_label
      closest_observation = abs(observation - self._
classification_a[0])
      if abs(observation - self._classification_b[0]) < closest_
observation:
        closest_class = self._classification_b_label
      return closest_class
```

From here, let's try changing our test a bit. Instead of dealing with variance and multiple observations, let's just test that the multiple observations do work.

We can now have a test that looks like the following:

```
def given_multiple_observations_for_two_classes_with_roughly_same_
variance_test ():
  classifier = NaiveBayes.Classifier()
  classifier.train(classification='a class', observation=0.0)
  classifier.train(classification='a class', observation=1.0)
  classifier.train(classification='a class', observation=75.0)
  classifier.train(classification='b class', observation=25)
  classifier.train(classification='b class', observation=99)
  classifier.train(classification='b class', observation=100)
  classification = classifier.classify(observation=25)
  assert classification == 'a class', "Should classify as the best fit
class."
  classification = classifier.classify(observation=75.0)
  assert classification == 'b class', "Should classify as the best fit
class."
```

This test setup is a little odd. By writing it like this, we make sure that the code has to take into account the previous data. If we just tested with the first two observations for both classes, the test would have passed with the current code. We can just classify on the basis of being closest to the mean for now. Let's code this up and see if we can get it working.

In order to get this test to pass, we just have to change the classify method to look like the following:

```
def classify(self, observation):
    if self._classification_a_label is None and self._
classification_b_label is None:
        return None
    elif self._classification_b_label is None:
      return self._classification_a_label
    else:
      closest_class = self._classification_a_label
      closest_observation = abs(observation - np.mean(self._
classification_a))
      if abs(observation - np.mean(self._classification_b)) < closest_
observation:
        closest_class = self._classification_b_label
    return closest_class
```

We're in a very different place compared to where we were heading before. Getting the tests to pass is much easier. The next thing we will add is the concept of probability, based on a Gaussian distribution. Let's start with a failing test:

```
def given_multiple_observations_for_two_classes_with_different_
variance_test():
  classifier = NaiveBayes.Classifier()
  classifier.train(classification='a class', observation=0.0)
  classifier.train(classification='a class', observation=1.0)
  classifier.train(classification='a class', observation=2.0)
  classifier.train(classification='b class', observation=50)
  classifier.train(classification='b class', observation=75)
  classifier.train(classification='b class', observation=100)
  classification = classifier.classify(observation=15)
  assert classification == 'b class', "Because of class b's variance
this should be class b."
  classification = classifier.classify(observation=2.5)
  assert classification == 'a class', "Should classify as class a
because of tight variance."
```

What we're really testing here is that if the a class has a really tight grouping; b class is pretty much distributed so that it's much easier to classify an observation as b class. Currently, we just look at the mean value of the training data, and see which mean value the observation is closest to. Because of this, when we run this test, we see that it fails.

We can make the following changes to get this test to pass:

```
def probability_of_data_given_class(self, observation, class_
observations):
    mean = np.mean(class_observations)
    variance = np.var(class_observations)
    p_data_given_class = 1/np.sqrt(2*np.pi*variance)*np.exp(-
0.5*((observation - mean)**2)/variance)
    return p_data_given_class


def classify(self, observation):
  if self._classification_a_label is None and self._classification_b_
label is None:
    return None
  elif self._classification_b_label is None:
    return self._classification_a_label
  else:
    closest_class = self._classification_a_label
    sum_of_probabilities = self.probability_of_data_given_
class(observation, self._classification_a) +\
```

```
                        self.probability_of_data_given_
    class(observation, self._classification_b)
        closest_observation = self.probability_of_data_given_
    class(observation, self._classification_a)/sum_of_probabilities
        if self.probability_of_data_given_class(observation, self._
    classification_b)/sum_of_probabilities > closest_observation:
            closest_class = self._classification_b_label
    return closest_class
```

We've made a few simplifying assumptions as well; to make the probability as simple as possible for now. How so? Let's look back at Bayes' Law.

Let $P(C_a | O) =$ Probability of a class given in the observation.

$$P(C_a | O) = \frac{P(O|C_a)P(C_a)}{P(O|C_a)P(C_a) + P(O|C_b)P(C_b)}$$

If we assume (as our tests so far have) that both of our classes are equally likely, then we can simplify the above equation to the following:

$$P(C_a | O) = \frac{P(O|C_a)}{P(O|C_a) + P(O|C_b)}$$

And this is how the code is written so far.

While the test that we were working on now passes, a different test failed. The test that failed is given_one_observation_for_two_classes_test. Why? Recall the formula for variance as $\sigma^2 = \sum \frac{(X - \mu)^2}{n}$. If we only have one value, then $X = \mu$ and our variance is zero. In the light of this, we should review the test and change it so that it makes sense in this context.

For now, let's change it to return none if any class only has one observation. The following is the updated test:

```
def given_one_observation_for_two_classes_test():
    classifier = NaiveBayes.Classifier()
    classifier.train(classification='a class', observation=0)
    classifier.train(classification='b class', observation=100)
    classification = classifier.classify(observation=23.2)
    assert classification is None, "Should not classify"
    classification = classifier.classify(observation=73.2)
    assert classification is None, "Should not classify"
```

It's still failing so now, I'll make it pass by just adding a new `if` to our classify method like the following:

```
def classify(self, observation):
  if self._classification_a_label is None and self._
classification_b_label is None:
    return None
  elif self._classification_b_label is None:
    return self._classification_a_label
  elif len(self._classification_a) == 1 or len(self._
classification_b) == 1:
    return None
  else:
    closest_class = self._classification_a_label
    sum_of_probabilities = self.probability_of_data_given_
class(observation, self._classification_a) +\
                          self.probability_of_data_given_
class(observation, self._classification_b)
    closest_observation = self.probability_of_data_given_
class(observation, self._classification_a)/sum_of_probabilities
    if self.probability_of_data_given_class(observation, self._
classification_b)/sum_of_probabilities > closest_observation:
      closest_class = self._classification_b_label
    return closest_class
```

After seeing the test pass, notice that it looks like we can refactor. Give it a shot and see if you can come up with something. The refactoring doesn't have an obvious solution that won't lead to a lot of broken, so let's hold off for now. We can always wait and see if it that becomes easier as we go ahead.

Next, we should test the probability calculations so that we can get them corrected theoretically. In order to test this, we will want to refactor our probability calculations to another method call that we can test in isolation.

I'll refactor the `classify` method to look like the following:

```
def _probability_of_each_class_given_data(self, observation, class_a_
data, class_b_data):
  sum_of_probabilities = self.probability_of_data_given_
class(observation, class_a_data) +\
                          self.probability_of_data_given_
class(observation, class_b_data)
  class_a_probability = self.probability_of_data_given_
class(observation, class_a_data)/sum_of_probabilities
  class_b_probability = self.probability_of_data_given_
class(observation, class_b_data)/sum_of_probabilities
  return (class_a_probability, class_b_probability)
```

```
def classify(self, observation):
  if self._classification_a_label is None and self._classification_b_
label is None:
    return None
  elif self._classification_b_label is None:
    return self._classification_a_label
  elif len(self._classification_a) <= 1 or len(self._classification_b)
<= 1:
    return None
  else:
    closest_class = self._classification_a_label
    p_of_A_given_data, p_of_B_given_data = self._probability_of_
each_class_given_data(observation, self._classification_a, self._
classification_b)
    if p_of_A_given_data > p_of_B_given_data:
      return self._classification_a_label
    else:
      return self._classification_b_label
```

Let's see if we can't concoct a test to give us a probability that matches Bayes Law even when the probability of the different classes differs. Do you happen to have an idea of one? Here's one possibility that's a bit tricky, but is exactly what we want:

```
def given_classes_of_different_likelihood_test():
  classifier = NaiveBayes.Classifier()
  observation = 3
  class_a_observations = [1,2,3,4,5]
  class_b_observations = [1,1,2,2,3,3,4,4,5,5]
  p_class_a, p_class_b = classifier._probability_of_each_class_given_
data(observation, class_a_observations, class_b_observations)
  assert p_class_b > p_class_a, "Should classify as class b when class
probability is taken into account."
```

Using the current implementation, class a and class b have a fifty-fifty chance given the data. Once we take into account the class probabilities (like we're supposed to), class b becomes way more likely (66 percent for class b versus 33 percent for class a). Remembering Bayes Law hopefully makes sense, because we've given class b more likelihood, as it becomes a more prevalent classification.

When I run this test, it fails as it should. Here is how I make it pass:

```
def _probability_of_each_class_given_data(self, observation, class_a_
data, class_b_data):
  p_class_a = len(class_a_data)/(1.0*(len(class_a_data) + len(class_b_
data)))
  p_class_b = len(class_b_data)/(1.0*(len(class_a_data) + len(class_b_
data)))
```

```
  sum_of_probabilities = self.probability_of_data_given_
class(observation, class_a_data) * p_class_a \
                        + self.probability_of_data_given_
class(observation, class_b_data)*p_class_b
  class_a_probability = self.probability_of_data_given_
class(observation, class_a_data)*p_class_a \
                      / sum_of_probabilities
  class_b_probability = self.probability_of_data_given_
class(observation, class_b_data)*p_class_b \
                      / sum_of_probabilities
  return (class_a_probability, class_b_probability)
```

By applying this, we're able to get the test swinging in the correct direction, and it finally passes.

What's left? Well at this point, we've got a Gaussian Naïve Bayes classifier that works with two classes and one-dimensional data. From here, we can break out to N classes or N dimensional data. Getting to N classes seems most useful, so let's tackle it.

For this test, we can just repurpose a previous test that was used for two classes. There's no law anywhere that states that once we've created a test, it's unchangeable. Let's use the `given_multiple_observations_for_two_classes_with_different_variance_test` test and add a third classification that won't affect the first two asserts, and then add a third assert to the test that we'll classify with the new class.

Here is the test that fails:

```
def given_multiple_observations_for_two_classes_with_different_
variance_test():
  classifier = NaiveBayes.Classifier()
  classifier.train(classification='a class', observation=0.0)
  classifier.train(classification='a class', observation=1.0)
  classifier.train(classification='a class', observation=2.0)

  classifier.train(classification='b class', observation=50)
  classifier.train(classification='b class', observation=75)
  classifier.train(classification='b class', observation=100)

  classifier.train(classification='c class', observation=0.0)
  classifier.train(classification='c class', observation=-1.0)
  classifier.train(classification='c class', observation=-2.0)
  classification = classifier.classify(observation=15)
  assert classification == 'b class', "Because of class b's variance
this should be class b."
  classification = classifier.classify(observation=2.5)
```

```
    assert classification == 'a class', "Should classify as class a
  because of tight variance."
    classification = classifier.classify(observation=-2.5)
    assert classification == 'c class', "Should classify as class c
  because it's the only negative one."
```

I actually expected this test to fail just by the addition of the training of a third class. Miraculously though, the code is so fixated on the two class cases that it completely ignores the third class. In order to get this working the way we expect, we're going to need to do some heavy refactoring. This is the ugly part that we got to do a while ago. The only difference is that instead of solving this problem plus all of the others that we've been working through, we now get to work on only this problem, and thus the whole process should be much clearer.

Here's the initial refactoring that touches everything but the probability methods:

```
import numpy as np
import collections

class Classifier:
  def __init__(self):
    self._classifications = collections.OrderedDict()
  def train(self, classification, observation):
    if not classification in self._classifications:
      self._classifications[classification] = []
    self._classifications[classification].append(observation)
  def probability_of_data_given_class(self, observation, class_
observations):
    mean = np.mean(class_observations)
    variance = np.var(class_observations)
    p_data_given_class = 1/np.sqrt(2*np.pi*variance)*np.exp(-
0.5*((observation - mean)**2)/variance)
    return p_data_given_class
  def _probability_of_each_class_given_data(self, observation,
class_a_data, class_b_data):
    p_class_a = len(class_a_data)/(1.0*(len(class_a_data) +
len(class_b_data)))
    p_class_b = len(class_b_data)/(1.0*(len(class_a_data) +
len(class_b_data)))
    sum_of_probabilities = self.probability_of_data_given_
class(observation, class_a_data) * p_class_a \
                           + self.probability_of_data_given_
class(observation, class_b_data)*p_class_b
    class_a_probability = self.probability_of_data_given_
class(observation, class_a_data)*p_class_a \
                         / sum_of_probabilities
```

```
        class_b_probability = self.probability_of_data_given_
class(observation, class_b_data)*p_class_b \
                          / sum_of_probabilities
        return (class_a_probability, class_b_probability)
    def _any_classes_are_too_small(self, classifications):
        for item in classifications.values():
            if len(item) <= 1:
                return True
        return False
    def classify(self, observation):
        if len(self._classifications.keys()) == 0:
            return None
        elif len(self._classifications.keys()) == 1:
            return self._classifications.keys()[0]
        elif self._any_classes_are_too_small(self._classifications):
            return None
        else:
            class_a = self._classifications.keys()[0]
            class_b = self._classifications.keys()[1]
            classifications_a = self._classifications[class_a]
            classifications_b = self._classifications[class_b]
            p_of_A_given_data, p_of_B_given_data = self._probability_
of_each_class_given_data(observation, classifications_a,
classifications_b)
            if p_of_A_given_data > p_of_B_given_data:
                return class_a
            else:
                return class_b
```

A lot of this is the same but different. One change that was made, which might seem odd, was the use of `OrderedDict`. The reason for this is that it allows the final test to pass by the way it orders the data, so that the first two classes in the test come first when we enumerate the data. Also notice that we should not be afraid to hard code some indexes in order to preserve the desired behavior. Rerunning our tests shows that everything still passes except the one assert that we're trying to get to pass.

Here is the finished class after making the tests pass:

```
import numpy as np

class Classifier:
    def __init__(self):
        self._classifications = {}
    def train(self, classification, observation):
        if not classification in self._classifications:
```

```
      self._classifications[classification] = []
    self._classifications[classification].append(observation)
  def probability_of_data_given_class(self, observation, class_
observations):
    mean = np.mean(class_observations)
    variance = np.var(class_observations)
    p_data_given_class = 1/np.sqrt(2*np.pi*variance)*np.exp(-
0.5*((observation - mean)**2)/variance)
    return p_data_given_class
  def _probability_of_each_class_given_data(self, observation,
classifications):
    all_observations = 1.0*sum([len(class_values) for class_values in
classifications.values()])
    class_probabilities = { class_label: len(classifications[class_
label])/all_observations
                            for class_label in classifications.keys()}
    sum_of_probabilities = sum([self.probability_of_data_given_
class(observation, classifications[class_label])
                                * class_probability
                                for class_label, class_probability in
class_probabilities.items()])
    probability_class_given_data = {}
    for class_label, observations in classifications.items():
      class_probability = self.probability_of_data_given_
class(observation, observations) \
        * class_probabilities[class_label] \
        / sum_of_probabilities
      probability_class_given_data[class_label] = class_probability
    return probability_class_given_data
  def _any_classes_are_too_small(self, classifications):
    for item in classifications.values():
      if len(item) <= 1:
        return True
    return False
  def classify(self, observation):
    if len(self._classifications.keys()) == 0:
      return None
    elif len(self._classifications.keys()) == 1:
      return self._classifications.keys()[0]
    elif self._any_classes_are_too_small(self._classifications):
      return None
    else:
      results = self._probability_of_each_class_given_
data(observation, self._classifications)
      return max(results.items(), key=lambda x: x[1])[0]
```

In the course of getting this test to pass, I also broke the test that validates the implementation of Bayes Law. The test just requires a little reworking of the interface, which I don't mind personally. This is the reworked version of that test:

```
def given_classes_of_different_likelihood_test():
  classifier = NaiveBayes.Classifier()
  observation = 3
  observations = {
    'class a': [1,2,3,4,5],
    'class b': [1,1,2,2,3,3,4,4,5,5]
  }
  results = classifier._probability_of_each_class_given_
data(observation, observations)
  print results
  assert results['class b'] > results['class a'], \
        "Should classify as class b when class probability is taken
into account."
```

It just needed the data to be packaged together with the class names.

We also removed `OrderedDict` from the classifier, since it was only a stopgap. Rerunning the tests after replacing it with a standard dictionary shows that everything works as planned.

Summary

In this chapter, we built up a Gaussian Naïve Bayes classifier, and ran into our first examples of truly necessary refactoring. We also saw how needing to make enormous changes in the code for a test is sometimes the result of trying to test too many concepts at once. We saw how backing up and rethinking test design can ultimately lead to a better and more elegantly designed piece of software as well.

In the next chapter, we'll apply this classifier to the real data, and see what it looks like to compare how different classifiers perform on the same data.

7
Optimizing by Choosing a New Algorithm

In this chapter, we'll dig into the heart of the problem that we have been preparing to solve—predicting which gender someone is from their height, weight, and BMI. We have built a N-class Gaussian Naïve Bayes classifier, but it only works on one dimension. This problem will require one addition of making our classifier support three dimensions. It may be tempting to modify it to support an arbitrary number of dimensions, but right now there wouldn't be any value to it. What's more, hard coding our class to work for three-dimensional input may help us save some time.

After this, we'll replace our custom classifier with a **Random Forest** classifier from scikit-learn. From there, we'll compare performance between the two classifiers and choose the one that we think works best.

Later in this chapter, we will be predicting the gender of a patient whose height, weight, and BMI is given. The data is stored in a simple CSV format. Our first step will be to improve our classifier to be able to handle a task like this.

Upgrading the classifier

In order to support the multi-dimensional data, my first step is to refactor the current tests to send their one-dimensional input as a one-dimensional tuple. This will set up our first test quite nicely.

After modifying the tests, you may be surprised when you rerun them to make sure that they break. Here is an example of a test modified that will pass observations as a multi-dimensional input:

```
def given_classes_of_different_likelihood_test():
  classifier = NaiveBayes.Classifier()
  observation = (3,)
  observations = {
    'class a': [(1,),(2,),(3,),(4,),(5,)],
    'class b': [(1,),(1,),(2,),(2,),(3,),(3,),(4,),(4,),(5,),(5,)]
  }
  results =
classifier._probability_of_each_class_given_data(observation,
observations)
  print results
  assert results['class b'] > results['class a'], "Should classify
as class b when class probability is taken into account."
```

You can see that every observation we pass into the algorithm is a one-dimensional tuple. What's surprising, though, is that rerunning our tests shows that all of our tests still pass. This makes our lives much easier. If you're wondering why, it's because of NumPy handling the multi-dimensional data in a very reasonable way.

For example, try running these two statements, and verify that they give you the same results:

```
np.sum([(1,),(1,),(1,)])
np.sum([1,1,1])
```

Next, we just need to make a new test to capture the behavior that we're looking for. Let's start with this:

```
def given_two_classes_with_two_dimension_inputs_test():
  classifier = NaiveBayes.Classifier()
  observation = (3,10)
  observations = {
    'class a': [(1,-1),(2,0),(3,-1),(4,1),(5,-1)],
    'class b': [(1,10),(2,5),(3,12),(4,10),(5,5)]
  }
  results =
classifier._probability_of_each_class_given_data(observation,
observations)
  print results
  assert results['class b'] > results['class a'], "Should classify
as class b because of dimension 2."
```

This test is set up in such a way that if the algorithm was looking just at the first dimension of the data, both the classes would have equally likely given the data. Only if the second dimension is being used correctly will we see the algorithm recommend class b over class a. When we run the tests, we see that this fails, but the way it fails is very interesting:

```
......E
====================================================================
ERROR: naive_bayes_tests.given_two_classes_with_two_dimension_inputs_t
est
--------------------------------------------------------------------
Traceback (most recent call last):
  File "/Library/Python/2.7/site-packages/nose-1.3.0-py2.7.egg/nose/ca
se.py", line 197, in runTest
    self.test(*self.arg)
  File "/Users/justin/Documents/Code/Machine-Learning-Test-by-Test/Cha
pter 7/naive_bayes_tests.py", line 76, in given_two_classes_with_two_d
imension_inputs_test
    assert results['class b'] > results['class a'], "Should classify a
s class b because of dimension 2."
ValueError: The truth value of an array with more than one element is
ambiguous. Use a.any() or a.all()
-------------------- >> begin captured stdout << ---------------------
{'class b': array([ 0.379657  ,  0.99954911]), 'class a': array([  6.2
0342995e-01,   4.50893925e-04])}

-------------------- >> end captured stdout << ----------------------


--------------------------------------------------------------------
Ran 7 tests in 0.157s

FAILED (errors=1)
```

Again, through the magic of NumPy, the algorithm is not failing catastrophically, but it is still giving us an undesired result. Our next step will be to get the test to fail in a controlled and expected way. In order to accomplish this, let's look at the algorithm. Specifically, this function gets called by the larger classification algorithm:

```python
def probability_of_data_given_class(self, observation,
class_observations):
    mean = np.mean(class_observations)
    variance = np.var(class_observations)
    p_data_given_class = 1/np.sqrt(2*np.pi*variance)*np.exp(-
0.5*((observation - mean)**2)/variance)
    return p_data_given_class
```

We can get everything to fail in the expected way if we can refactor this code to only look at the first dimension of the data and its observation. We can make this happen like the following code:

```
def probability_of_data_given_class(self, observation,
class_observations):
    mean = np.mean(map(lambda x: x[0], class_observations))
    variance = np.var(map(lambda x: x[0], class_observations))
    p_data_given_class = 1/np.sqrt(2*np.pi*variance)*np.exp(-
0.5*((observation[0] - mean)**2)/variance)
    return p_data_given_class
```

When we run the test now, we see the following output:

```
......F
================================================================
FAIL: naive_bayes_tests.given_two_classes_with_two_dimension_inputs_te
st
----------------------------------------------------------------
Traceback (most recent call last):
  File "/Library/Python/2.7/site-packages/nose-1.3.0-py2.7.egg/nose/ca
se.py", line 197, in runTest
    self.test(*self.arg)
  File "/Users/justin/Documents/Code/Machine-Learning-Test-by-Test/Cha
pter 7/naive_bayes_tests.py", line 76, in given_two_classes_with_two_d
imension_inputs_test
    assert results['class b'] > results['class a'], "Should classify a
s class b because of dimension 2."
AssertionError: Should classify as class b because of dimension 2.
-------------------- >> begin captured stdout << ----------------------
{'class b': 0.5, 'class a': 0.5}

-------------------- >> end captured stdout << ----------------------


----------------------------------------------------------------
Ran 7 tests in 0.151s

FAILED (failures=1)
```

Notice where we print out the results of the test. It says the following:

```
{'class b': 0.5, 'class a': 0.5}
```

This shows us that the test is now failing for the right reason. As the algorithm is only looking at the data in the first dimension, both of the classes seem just as likely. Now, in the next change that we make, let's figure out how to get this to pass.

The way to generalize Bayes' Law is to just multiply the probabilities of each dimension of our input together. In this way, an observation of (3,10) can be used to find the probability of the given class $x1 = 3$ and $x2 = 10$. To state it more formally, we're looking at the following message: $P(C \mid x_0, x_1, \ldots, x_n)$. This breaks down mathematically like the following:

$$P(C \mid x_0, x_1, \ldots, x_n) = \frac{P(C) * P(x_0, x_1, \ldots, x_n \mid C)}{P(x_0, x_1, \ldots, x_n)}$$

The entire method that we've been working with calculates the following: $P(x_0, x_1, \ldots, x_n \mid C)$. This is equivalent to the conditional probability of the following:

$$P(x_0, x_1, \ldots, x_n \mid C) = P(x_0 \mid C) * P(x_1 \mid C) *, \ldots, P(x_n \mid C)$$

This is exactly what this code needs to translate into in order to pass our test. The divisions won't happen here though. It eventually takes care of itself once we've found the conditional probability of each class. The reason being that it really just serves to normalize our probability to lie between zero and one inclusively.

Here is the updated code, where we multiply the probabilities of each dimension of the input by one another to come up with our result:

```
def probability_of_data_given_class(self, observation,
class_observations):
  lists_of_observations = zip(*class_observations)
  probabilities = []
  for class_observation_index in
range(len(lists_of_observations)):
      some_class_observations = lists_of_observations[class_
observation_index]
      the_observation = observation[class_observation_index]
      mean = np.mean(some_class_observations)
      variance = np.var(some_class_observations)
      p_data_given_class = 1/np.sqrt(2*np.pi*variance)*np.exp(-
0.5*((the_observation - mean)**2)/variance)
      probabilities.append(p_data_given_class)
  return reduce(operator.mul,probabilities,1)
```

The first line of our function serves to reorganize the data from being by the rows of input values to being by the columns of input values. In this way, each column maps to a dimension of our input value, and we can easily compute our probabilities. The middle portion is largely the same with some additional variables to index through our input dimensions. The last line is equivalent to the following equation:

$$P(x_0, x_1, \ldots, x_n \mid C) = P(x_0 \mid C) * P(x_1 \mid C) *, \ldots, P(x_n \mid C)$$

We multiply all of the probabilities together to find the probability of seeing each bit of data given in the class that we're evaluating. Just to make extra certain that this is working, let's add another interesting test case and make sure that it passes as well.

Here's one that should be a gimme:

```
def given_two_classes_with_identical_two_dimension_inputs_test():
    classifier = NaiveBayes.Classifier()
    observation = (3,10)
    observations = {
        'class a': [(1,10),(2,5),(3,12),(4,10),(5,5)],
        'class b': [(1,10),(2,5),(3,12),(4,10),(5,5)]
    }
    results =
classifier._probability_of_each_class_given_data(observation,
observations)
    print results
    assert results['class a'] == 0.5, "There should be 50/50 chance
of class a"
    assert results['class b'] == 0.5, "There should be 50/50 chance
of class b"
```

This test passes right off the bat, which is a good sign. Next, let's try out our classifier with some real data and see if we get some realistic results.

Applying our classifier

Now we put the pedal to the metal. Can we classify gender by height, weight, and BMI? We will get our data from the Kaggle competition at https://www.kaggle.com/c/pf2012-diabetes/data.

We'll be using the SyncPatient and SyncTranscript data. You can look up the details regarding these datasets in the associated data dictionary. The examples that follow are placed in the data files, in a directory named `data`. The files have also been renamed from `SyncPatient.csv` and `SyncTranscript.csv` to `training_SyncPatient.csv` and `training_SyncTranscript.csv` respectively.

Our first step will be to create a harness that will let us explore our data to make sure that it seems reasonable. Before we do this, we should create a new method on our Naïve Bayes class that can show us what the internal data looks like. This is the code that should be added to your Naïve Bayes class:

```python
def _calculate_model_parameters(self):
  class_metrics = {}
  for class_label, data in self._classifications.items():
    class_metrics[class_label] = []
    columnar_data = zip(*data)
    for column in columnar_data:
      class_metrics[class_label].append({
        "mean": np.mean(column),
        "variance": np.var(column)
      })
```

This is the code that's written to be the harness in our test file that will use this new method:

```python
import pandas, pprint
import numpy as np
def given_real_data_test():
  patients =
pandas.DataFrame.from_csv('./data/training_SyncPatient.csv').reset_
index()
  transcripts =
pandas.DataFrame.from_csv('./data/training_SyncTranscript.csv').reset_
index()
  transcripts = transcripts[transcripts['Height'] > 0]
  transcripts = transcripts[transcripts['Weight'] > 0]
  transcripts = transcripts[transcripts['BMI'] > 0]
  joined_df = patients.merge(transcripts, on='PatientGuid',
how='inner')
  final_df =
joined_df.groupby('PatientGuid').first().reset_index()

  female_set =
final_df.ix[np.random.choice(final_df[final_df['Gender']=='F'].index,
500)]
```

```
   male_set =
final_df.ix[np.random.choice(final_df[final_df['Gender']=='M'].index,
500)]
   training_data = map(lambda x: (x[2], (x[8], x[9],x[10]))),
female_set.values)
   training_data += map(lambda x: (x[2], (x[8], x[9],x[10]))),
male_set.values)
   #print training_data
   classifier = NaiveBayes.Classifier()
   for class_label, input_data in training_data:
     classifier.train(classification=class_label,
observation=input_data)

   # Manual verification
   pprint.pprint(classifier._calculate_model_parameters())

   # Men
   print "Men"
   print classifier.classify(observation=(71.3, 210.0, 23.509))
   print classifier.classify(observation=(66.0, 268.8,
27.241999999999997))
   print classifier.classify(observation=(65.0, 284.0, 30.616))
   print "Women"
   print classifier.classify(observation=(60.5, 151.0, 29.002))
   print classifier.classify(observation=(60.0, 148.0, 28.901))
   print classifier.classify(observation=(60.0, 134.923,
26.346999999999998))
   assert False
```

What this does is pull in the data from the test file, clean it up since there are some null values (the lines where we make sure height, weight, and BMI are all >0), and then randomly select a batch of 500 men and 500 women to train the classifier. Once the classifier is trained, it outputs the mean and variance for each class and each dimension of the input so that we can have an idea of what a men and women look like in this dataset. We've also hardcoded it to always fail so that we can see how well it does, and why it fails when it does.

Here's what the output looks like on my screen:

```
-------------------- >> begin captured stdout << --------------------
{'F': [{'mean': 63.696218000000002, 'variance': 12.162890218475999},
       {'mean': 164.53548800000002, 'variance': 1653.804317381856},
       {'mean': 28.529872000000001, 'variance': 46.7721001276159922}],
 'M': [{'mean': 69.163201999999984, 'variance': 13.695821797196},
       {'mean': 198.34125400000002, 'variance': 1589.8334884054839},
       {'mean': 29.133306000000001, 'variance': 28.673036156363999}]}
Men
M
M
M
Women
F
F
F


-------------------- >> end captured stdout << --------------------


--------------------------------------------------------------------
Ran 10 tests in 1.290s

FAILED (failures=1)
```

The input is structured in such a way that the positions are consistent with how we have fed the data to it. Since we're giving it height, weight, and BMI, the previous means and variances follow this pattern. As an example, the average height for the females was 63 inches, the average weight was 164 lbs, and the average BMI was 69, and so on. This tells us how our classifier has defined male and female, in terms of these three variables.

In the following bit, I have handpicked some obvious men and women from the larger dataset (because they meet the definition of male/female established previously, and because they are tagged as men and women in the dataset). M and F are the classifications that the classifier gives them.

With obvious data, this is doing pretty well. Now, it's time to see how accurate it is over an entire dataset. In order to do this, let's set up the following cross validation test harness:

```
def quantify_classifier_accuracy_test():
    # Load and clean up the data
    patients =
pandas.DataFrame.from_csv('./data/training_SyncPatient.csv').reset_
index()
```

```
    transcripts =
pandas.DataFrame.from_csv('./data/training_SyncTranscript.csv').reset_
index()
    transcripts = transcripts[transcripts['Height'] > 0]
    transcripts = transcripts[transcripts['Weight'] > 0]
    transcripts = transcripts[transcripts['BMI'] > 0]
    joined_df = patients.merge(transcripts, on='PatientGuid',
how='inner')
    final_df =
joined_df.groupby('PatientGuid').first().reset_index()
    total_set = final_df.ix[np.random.choice(final_df.index, 7000,
replace=False)]

    # Partition development and cross-validation datasets
    training_count = 2000
    training_data = map(lambda x: (x[2], (x[8], x[9], x[10])),
total_set.values[:training_count])
    cross_validate_data = map(lambda x: (x[2], (x[8], x[9],
x[10])), total_set.values[training_count:])

    # Train the classifier on the training data.
    classifier = NaiveBayes.Classifier()
    for class_label, input_data in training_data:
      classifier.train(classification=class_label,
observation=input_data)

    # Test how well the classifier generalizes.
    number_correct = 0
    number_tested = 0
    for class_label, input_data in cross_validate_data:
      number_tested += 1
      assigned_class = classifier.classify(observation=input_data)
      if class_label == assigned_class:
        number_correct += 1

    correct_rate = number_correct/(1.*number_tested)
    print "Correct rate: {0}, Total: {1}".format(correct_rate,
number_tested)
    assert correct_rate > 0.6, "Should be significantly better
than random."
    pprint.pprint(classifier._calculate_model_parameters())
    assert False
```

Notice the assert at the very end. To start with, lets just look for a better-than-random performance, which we call 60 percent accuracy. Also, notice that we are not forcing the classifier to be trained on exactly 50 percent male/female. This is so that if there are some data points that we need to classify which are difficult to really tell the difference of a man from woman, we can choose whoever makes up the largest proportion of the data. Let's run the test and see how it goes. Here are the results of the test that you run (your results will differ):

```
        assert False
AssertionError:
-------------------- >> begin captured stdout << --------------------
Correct rate: 0.7936, Total: 5000
{'F': [{'mean': 63.595020512820511, 'variance': 16.240506356844183},
       {'mean': 166.52739487179485, 'variance': 1994.8113539380934},
       {'mean': 36.486458119658124, 'variance': 30504.141355082436}],
 'M': [{'mean': 69.002157831325292, 'variance': 24.52815720761939},
       {'mean': 198.35300722891566, 'variance': 1702.1144923903094},
       {'mean': 37.555443373493979, 'variance': 26226.362753873291}]}

-------------------- >> end captured stdout << --------------------


-----------------------------------------------------------------------
Ran 11 tests in 20.608s

FAILED (failures=1)
```

Wow! We got 80 percent accuracy right out of the box. This is not too shabby. This is high enough that we won't spend any further time tuning the algorithm. Instead, we'll just move on to trying the same classification task using a completely different approach: Random Forests.

Upgrading to Random Forest

We did a lot of great work in building up the classifier. Naïve Bayes, while usually not a bad choice, is typically never the best choice of classifier. Next, we'll try comparing its performance to an algorithm that is usually a great choice: Random Forest. Unlike the Naïve Bayes algorithm, we won't be implementing this by hand.

The reason has very little to do with the complication and more to do with the fact that it's better practice to avoid the leg work and the time cost of rolling your own algorithms by hand. A lot of sections in this book have covered how to roll your own algorithms in a test-driven manner, so you have the tools to do so if need be. The rest of this book will cover more of a test-driven approach in using the third-party libraries.

To get started, we can build a wrapper class around sklearn's functionality so that we can keep the same interface that we already have, but leverage the power of a third-party library. We should start with the same test framework that we've used to get the accuracy of our Naïve Bayes classifier. We can then change it to use our as-of-yet not developed Random Forest classifier.

You might wonder why we don't start with the smallest and simplest test possible. Well, here we aren't testing the algorithm, we're just testing our usage of sklearn in such a way that it gives us a good answer. It is possible that we might want to test certain special cases and make sure that we handle them consistently, but this isn't critical for our purposes.

Here's where we can start:

```python
import RandomForest
def random_forest_adapter_test():
    # Load and clean up the data
    patients =
pandas.DataFrame.from_csv('./data/training_SyncPatient.csv').reset_
index()
    transcripts =
pandas.DataFrame.from_csv('./data/training_SyncTranscript.csv').reset_
index()
    transcripts = transcripts[transcripts['Height'] > 0]
    transcripts = transcripts[transcripts['Weight'] > 0]
    transcripts = transcripts[transcripts['BMI'] > 0]
    joined_df = patients.merge(transcripts, on='PatientGuid',
how='inner')
    final_df =
joined_df.groupby('PatientGuid').first().reset_index()
    total_set = final_df.ix[np.random.choice(final_df.index, 7000,
replace=False)]

    # Partition development and cross-validation datasets
    training_count = 500
    training_data = map(lambda x: (x[2], (x[8], x[9], x[10])),
total_set.values[:training_count])
    cross_validate_data = map(lambda x: (x[2], (x[8], x[9],
x[10])), total_set.values[training_count:])

    # Train the classifier on the training data.
    classifier = RandomForest.Classifier()
    classifier.batch_train(training_data)

    # Test how well the classifier generalizes.
    number_correct = 0
```

```
    number_tested = 0
    for class_label, input_data in cross_validate_data:
      number_tested += 1
      assigned_class = classifier.classify(observation=input_data)
      if class_label == assigned_class:
        number_correct += 1

    correct_rate = number_correct/(1.*number_tested)
    print "Correct rate: {0}, Total: {1}".format(correct_rate,
number_tested)
    assert correct_rate > 0.6, "Should be significantly better
than random."
```

The cross-validation step checks that we still have good results if we run our model on the data we didn't use to train it with. The bold code is the only bit that has changed. sklearn's `RandomForest` takes all of its data at once, so we need to use a new method called `batch_train`. It will take in data in the same form as before, but it will be batched into a list. Once we get this working, we can refactor our other code to use a method like this instead of what we were doing.

As a part of getting the wrapper in place, we just let it always return null. We get the following output when running the tests:

```
--------------------- >> begin captured stdout << ---------------------
Correct rate: 0.0, Total: 5000

--------------------- >> end captured stdout << ---------------------


-----------------------------------------------------------------------
Ran 12 tests in 21.813s

FAILED (errors=1)
```

Out of 5,000 different attempts, it didn't get anything correct. This makes sense, since we're always just returning `None`. Let's see how this changes if we hardcode report `M` as the class. By predicting everything as `M`, we get almost 44 percent accuracy. Next, let's hook this up to sklearn.

This is the code, which does exactly it:

```
from sklearn.ensemble import RandomForestClassifier
class Classifier:
  def __init__(self):
    self._forest = RandomForestClassifier()
    self._model = None
  def batch_train(self, observations):
    class_labels = map(lambda x: x[0], observations)
```

```
      class_inputs = map(lambda x: x[1], observations)
      self._model = self._forest.fit(class_inputs, class_labels)
    def classify(self, observation):
      return self._model.predict(observation)
```

By hooking up to sklearn, we get an accuracy of 77 percent, which is almost the same as our Naïve Bayes implementation. Next, let's try fiddling with things to see if we can squeeze any extra accuracy out of our model. We can go here to find all of the different parameters, we can try tuning it at `http://scikit-learn.org/stable/` `modules/generated/sklearn.ensemble.RandomForestClassifier.html`.

The first thing we can try to change is the `max_features` parameter in the constructor of the classifier. By default, it is set to 10. This means that the Random Forest will have 10 trees in it. Lets try turning this up to 100. After rerunning the test, we see that performance hits just over 79 percent. Increasing `n_estimators` to 500 reduces the accuracy to around 75 percent. Trying a few other options between 0 and 100, and just over 100, gives either the same accuracy or worse.

We have one last loose end. We need to get the interfaces of our Naïve Bayes and Random Forest classifiers to line up. In order to do so, we can just change a pre-existing test using the training method that trains incrementally to the batch method that we use for Random Forest.

This test works well for our needs:

```
def
given_multiple_observations_for_two_classes_with_roughly_same_
variance_test():
  classifier = NaiveBayes.Classifier()
  classifier.batch_train([('a class',(0.0,)),
                          ('a class',(1.0,)),
                          ('a class',(75.0,)),
                          ('b class',(25,)),
                          ('b class',(99,)),
                          ('b class',(100,))])

  classification = classifier.classify(observation=(25,))
  assert classification == 'a class', "Should classify as the best
fit class."
  classification = classifier.classify(observation=(75.0,))
  assert classification == 'b class', "Should classify as the best
fit class."
```

When you first run this test, you will, of course, see that it fails. Getting it to pass is extremely simple, though. We just implement this on the `NaiveBayes.Classifier` class:

```
def batch_train(self, observations):
    for label, observation in observations:
        self.train(label, observation)
```

Summary

In this instance, it looks like our home grown Naïve Bayes just slightly outperforms Random Forest with some quick tuning and tweaking. We have a deep understanding of creating Gaussian Naïve Bayes classifiers, and we've seen how little we need to understand Random Forests in order to use them as a black box.

In the next chapter, we're going to explore and further dig into libraries like sklearn. We'll use TDD and our unit test tool as a way to build documentation and learn about the code. We'll continue working with classes, and we'll find new ways of testing that we're using sklearn and other third party libraries the way we think we are.

8
Exploring scikit-learn Test First

We've explored building the machine learning models from scratch, we've learned about tuning a classifier, and we've understood the usage of a third-party library, all in a test-driven manner. We haven't really talked about building a full system around these techniques. When we say "full system", we're talking about something that promotes sustainable and controlled software development. If we build an entire machine learning project and aren't careful about it, we can end up being tightly coupled with a third-party library. This is a bad thing because this could put us in a situation where changing the underlying library could mean we have to rewrite the entire system.

Why is this important? After we create our first model that is successful what are our options for further improvement down the road? If we chose a great library then we'll have many options for tuning our model and probably even many options for other models. Do we really want to be tied to one machine-learning library forever? No, of course not. We want a system that can grow over time as we learn new techniques or new libraries are created.

In this chapter, we will build a system that can use either the Naïve Bayes or Random Forest classifiers that are available with the flip of a switch. You could think of this as possibly being the start of building a platform that will enable you to continuously improve your model quality. In places, we'll use **TDD** to learn about how to use the other options in the scikit-learn library. Then, we can get them added into the system at large to have more classification options to choose from.

In order to explore the options at our fingertips and how to use them, we will use TDD to build a sort of living documentation of how to interact with the different components of the library.

Let's start by discussing some of the core concepts that have been hinted at.

Test-driven design

Until now, we've left the concept of **test-driven design** (TDD) out of discussion. Now that we have some experience in applying TDD to concrete problems, it's a great time to discuss some of the less concrete aspects of it.

Test-driven design has a notion that the biggest value we see from TDD is the result of the code that we design. It's completely fine if this is not immediately obvious. Think about it like this: how does code that is designed with the help of TDD differ from code that is designed up front, and then written? The code designed with the help of TDD is done incrementally, and in response to how effectively the current design is solving problems. Think of your tests as the first "user" of your code. If the code is difficult to test, then it is also probably difficult to use.

We saw an example of this when we built our Naïve Bayes classifier. We were heading down a route that was becoming increasingly difficult to test. Instead of charging ahead without testing, we took a step back, rethought our approach, and arrived at a simpler design than where we were initially. TDD really should be thought of as a subset of test-driven design. It is quite possible to make a mess using TDD, but if one is listening to the feedback that their testing is giving them, and responding to it with refactoring and incremental design, then they are well on their way to practicing test-driven design. There is a great article on the subject by Dr. Dobbs at `http://www.drdobbs.com/architecture-and-design/test-driven-design/240168102`. The main take away is that a key value of testing is the incremental development of an optimal architecture.

Let's make this concrete by working with some of our code from the previous chapters. We'll bring back our Naïve Bayes and Random Forest classifiers, and make a system where we can switch between the two models with very little effort.

Planning our journey

TDD is a way to incrementally design our code, but this doesn't mean that we can stop thinking about it. Getting some idea of how we want to approach the problem can actually be quite useful, as long as we're prepared to leave behind our preconceptions if it doesn't prove to be a testable design.

Let's take a moment to review the Naïve Bayes and Random Forest classifiers. What are the methods/functions that they have in common? It looks like `batch_train` and `classify` have the same signature, and both appear on both classes. Python doesn't have the concept of interfaces similar to what Java or C# have, but if it did have, we might have an interface that would look like the following:

```
class Classifier:
  def batch_train(self, observations):
    pass
  def classify(self, observation):
    pass
```

In programming languages such as C# and Java, **interfaces** are useful for defining the methods that one expects a class to have, but this happens without specifying any implementation details. Here, we use a stripped down class definition to give us an idea of the necessary interface for us to have a working classifier. In other words, this system that will switch back and forth between these two different approaches will need to depend on this common interface.

What we want to be able to do is train and evaluate our models on the same input and test sets and then have the best model used to make predictions in "production" (pseudo-production). While you're building up the class that will decide which implementation we will use, you will notice that you won't even need to use our current classifiers. We'll just create a couple of fake classifiers with known behavior so that we can test that this classifier chooser can be shown to make reasonable choices. This is extra work though. The reason for approaching problems in this way is to keep our tests simple. Testing each component of our system in isolation means that we just need to test the features of each component, and not the cross product of features that would occur by using our components in concert with each other.

Creating a classifier chooser (it needs to run tests to evaluate classifier performance)

First, let's test our most basic scenario, where we've given the `ClassifierChooser` no input whatsoever, and have asked it to classify some input. Let's make this a case that ends with an exception:

```
@nose.tools.raises(NoClassifierOptionsException)
def given_no_model_options_test():
    classifier_chooser = ClassifierChooser()
    classifier_chooser.classify([42])
```

The `ClassifierChooser` class has the responsibility of choosing the appropriate classifier for the usage. This design means that the calling code doesn't need to be concerned with all of the different types of classifiers that might be used. Instead, it just knows the usage of this one class, and everything will work just fine. To start with, we will use it with two extremely simple classifiers. One will always predict *true*, and one will always predict *false*. This will allow us to make sure that the `ClassifierChooser` makes good decisions, and makes the scenarios much easier to understand, because they will fairly be black and white.

This first test just makes sure that if we don't provide any classifiers for the chooser to use, then it fails with a meaningful exception. In order to make this pass, we first need to create this exception so that the test fails for the right reason. We do so by implementing enough of the class that we get an error about the exception not being thrown. After implementing the most basic class and exception (as well as saving the code as `choosey.py`) we'll see an error that says the following:

```
AssertionError: given_no_model_options_test() did not raise
NoClassifierOptionsException
```

We'll fix the test with the following code:

```
class NoClassifierOptionsException(Exception):
    pass


class ClassifierChooser:
    def classify(self, input):
        raise NoClassifierOptionsException()
```

As we think about the next test, we should think about how we'd like to use this class. Initially, I was thinking an overall test might look like the following:

```
from choosey import *


def given_two_models_and_one_knows_the_answers():
    classifier_chooser = ClassifierChooser()
    classifier_chooser.choose_from([AlwaysRightClassifier(),
AlwaysWrongClassifier()])
    classifier_chooser.test_with(input=[1, 0, 1, 0],
                                 labels=[1, 0, 1, 0])
    classifier_chooser.train_with(input=[1, 0, 1, 0],
                                  labels=[1, 0, 1, 0])
    assert classifier_chooser.classify([1]) == 1, "should guess
correctly because it chose the best classifier."
    assert classifier_chooser.classify([0]) == 0, "should guess
correctly because it chose the best classifier."
```

This was my preconception of the end design of the software. When I started thinking about this, a big value helped me see all of the information that we'll need to do about what we want. To be able to classify some input, we need at least one classifier option, some data to test with, some data to train with, and a way to classify an input. If we need all of this information, our object will guide us to use it correctly, and it won't make us have to guess what's required and see whether it works or not.

After some thought, we find that we really don't have a valid object until we have all of this data. As a result, we should change our first test by raising the exception on the instantiation of the class without the required information. The constructor needs to make sure we have appropriate data to use. Let's change our test to look like the following and rerun our tests:

```
@nose.tools.raises(NoClassifierOptionsException)
def given_no_model_options_test():
    classifier_chooser = ClassifierChooser()
```

We now have a failing test that can be fixed by just throwing our exception in the constructor. Before refactoring the code, we will have something like the following:

```
class ClassifierChooser:
    def __init__(self):
        raise NoClassifierOptionsException()
    def classify(self, input):
        raise NoClassifierOptionsException()
```

The important part is that we got the test to pass in the minimum number of steps even when our class could use some refactoring. Let's take this opportunity to refactor the test by dropping the classify method. This leaves us with the following:

```
class ClassifierChooser:
    def __init__(self):
        raise NoClassifierOptionsException()
```

We've refactored, so now let's rerun our tests. Everything passes so let's move on and get to the meat of this problem. For the next test, let's consider the simplest scenario where we can see some classification taking place. Here's one such scenario:

```
def given_a_single_classifier_option_that_does_not_require_training_
test():
    classifier_chooser = ClassifierChooser(classifier_
options=AlwaysTrueClassifier())
    predicted_label = classifier_chooser.classify(42)
    assert predicted_label, "Should be true because that's all our
classifier predicts."
```

In this scenario, since we only have one classifier, there is nothing to compare it with, so we don't need to test its performance. Also, since it always just predicts true, it doesn't need to be trained. Notice that even though we know we'll need/want multiple classifier options soon, we start without the concept of having a list of them. The same thing is applicable for the input to the `classify` function. Let's get this test to pass. First things first, let's create our `AlwaysTrueClassifier`:

We can create the following quick test to define its behavior:

```
def given_an_AlwaysTrueClassifier_test():
    classifier = AlwaysTrueClassifier()
    predicted_label = classifier.classify(55)
    assert predicted_label == 1, "Should always predict one."
```

This is easy enough to make pass. We just create the following tiny class:

```
class AlwaysTrueClassifier:
    def classify(self, input):
        return 1
```

Great, now we can move on to the main test failure. The following code solves the failing test even though it's cheating:

```
class ClassifierChooser:
    def __init__(self, classifier_options=None):
        if classifier_options is None:
            raise NoClassifierOptionsException()
    def classify(self, input):
        return True
```

It is completely understandable if this "cheating" seems ridiculous. We keep doing these crazy broken solutions because they help to solidify our test suite. The more we do such silly things, the less our test suite assumes about the developer writing code. It will then more actively guard someone from failure. The next test will force us to fix this deceit:

```
def given_a_different_single_classifier_option_that_does_not_require_
training_test():
    classifier_chooser = ClassifierChooser(classifier_options=AlwaysFa
lseClassifier())
    predicted_label = classifier_chooser.classify(42)
    assert not predicted_label, "Should be false because that's
all our classifier predicts."
```

It's basically the same test that we ran before, but this one will make us add some functionality to our `ClassifierChooser`. We can get the test to pass with the following code:

```
class AlwaysTrueClassifier:
    def classify(self, input):
        return 1


class ClassifierChooser:
    def __init__(self, classifier_options=None):
        if classifier_options is None:
            raise NoClassifierOptionsException()
        else:
            self._classifier_options = classifier_options
    def classify(self, input):
        return self._classifier_options.classify(None)
```

We cheated yet again! We're not actually passing the input to our chosen classifier. We can fix this by changing the way we do our testing. Instead of using classifiers that always return a constant value, we can create a single classifier that returns the value input into it. Let's write a test and implement it:

```
def given_a_CopyCatClassifier_test():
    classifier = CopyCatClassifier()
    input_value = 12.5
    predicted_label = classifier.classify(input_value)
    assert predicted_label == input_value, "Should predict the
value to be what the input is."

    input_value = 77
    predicted_label = classifier.classify(input_value)
    assert predicted_label == input_value, "Should predict the
value to be what the input is."
```

The code for the `CopyCatClassifier` looks like the following:

```
class CopyCatClassifier:
  def batch_train(self, observations):
      pass
  def classify(self, input):
      return input
```

We can take some larger steps in the less important areas in the interest of brevity. Now that we have a `CopyCatClassifier`, let's have our tests use it, and see if we can't make our test suite a bit simpler as a result. We can rework our second test to use this new classifier like the following:

```
def given_a_single_classifier_option_that_does_not_require_training_
test():
    classifier_chooser = ClassifierChooser(classifier_
options=CopyCatClassifier())
    input_value = 42
    predicted_label = classifier_chooser.classify(input_value)
    assert predicted_label == input_value, "Should predict input
value."
```

It definitely fails. Let's see if passing our input value down to the chosen classifier fixes our tests. Let's change the `ClassifierChooser` to look like the following:

```
class ClassifierChooser:
    def __init__(self, classifier_options=None):
        if classifier_options is None:
            raise NoClassifierOptionsException()
        else:
            self._classifier_options = classifier_options
    def classify(self, input):
        return self._classifier_options.classify(input)
```

After this makes everything pass, you may notice now that we don't need the `AlwaysTrueClassifier` or the `AlwaysFalseClassifier`. We can just add one more test case and delete the other tests like the following:

```
def given_a_single_classifier_option_that_does_not_require_training_
test():
    classifier_chooser = ClassifierChooser(classifier_
options=CopyCatClassifier())
    input_value = 42
    predicted_label = classifier_chooser.classify(input_value)
    assert predicted_label == input_value, "Should predict input
value."

    input_value = 11
    predicted_label = classifier_chooser.classify(input_value)
    assert predicted_label == input_value, "Should predict input
value."
```

Alright, next let's get this code working with a list of classifier options. This will require us to also test each classifier, compare their performance, and choose the best performing classifier to use for the classification. Let's see what's the simplest test that we can get away with. If we still had the `AlwaysTrueClassifier` and `AlwaysFalseClassifier`, we could get away with not having to train anything, and just focus on getting our test to use more than one classifier. Let's bring them back (along with their tests).

Next, we can set up the simplest test we can think of that will drive us to something valuable:

```
def given_multiple_classifier_options_test():
    classifier_chooser = ClassifierChooser(classifier_options_list=[
            AlwaysTrueClassifier(),
            AlwaysFalseClassifier()
        ],
        test_input=78,
        test_label=1)
    predicted_label = classifier_chooser.classify(0)
    assert predicted_label == 1, "Should choose best classifier
option to classify with."
```

We can get this test to pass by not worrying about the accuracy of the test, and instead viewing it as a true/false test. The first classifier to get the single question right gets chosen. Here is how we can code it up:

```
class ClassifierChooser:
    def __init__(self,
                    classifier_options=None,
                    classifier_options_list=None,
                    test_label=None,
                    test_input=None):
        if not classifier_options_list is None:
            self._classifier_options_list =
classifier_options_list
            for classifier in classifier_options_list:
                predicted_label = classifier.classify(test_input)
                if predicted_label == test_label:
                    self._classifier_options = classifier
        elif classifier_options is None:
            raise NoClassifierOptionsException()
        else:
            self._classifier_options = classifier_options
    def classify(self, input):
        return self._classifier_options.classify(input)
```

Our test passes, so let's look for the refactoring opportunities. There seems to be a lot of complexity here, and it seems to be largely caused by the fact that we have a separate parameter for a single classifier option versus having multiple classifier options. What if we refactor the code to have separate static methods for multiple classifier options or a single one? Perhaps, it can reduce the number of ifs in our code.

Let's start by adding the following static method:

```
@staticmethod
def create_with_single_classifier_option(classifier_option):
    return ClassifierChooser(classifier_options_list=[classifier_
option])
```

Next, let's refactor the test that has a single classifier option, and rerun our test suite to make sure the tests still pass:

```
def given_a_single_classifier_option_that_does_not_require_training_
test():
    classifier_chooser =
ClassifierChooser.create_with_single_classifier_
option(CopyCatClassifier())
    input_value = 42
    predicted_label = classifier_chooser.classify(input_value)
    assert predicted_label == input_value, "Should predict input
value."
```

All of our tests still pass, so let's move on to the next refactoring. Next, we can try to remove the classifier_options parameter in the constructor. Refactoring to this keeps the tests passing:

```
class ClassifierChooser:
    def __init__(self,
                 classifier_options_list=None,
                 test_label=None,
                 test_input=None):
        if not classifier_options_list is None:
            self._classifier_options_list =
classifier_options_list
            for classifier in classifier_options_list:
                predicted_label = classifier.classify(test_input)
                if predicted_label == test_label:
                    self._classifier_options = classifier
        else:
            raise NoClassifierOptionsException()
```

Now, it's pretty obvious that we can get along without even defaulting the `classifier_options_list` parameter. We will need to expect a different error but it's easy enough. Let's modify our test to just look for an exception. Refactoring has worked our constructor into the following shape:

```
def __init__(self,
             classifier_options_list,
             test_label=None,
             test_input=None):
    for classifier in classifier_options_list:
        predicted_label = classifier.classify(test_input)
        if predicted_label == test_label:
            self._classifier_options = classifier
```

All of our tests are passing, but at this point, it's not entirely obvious why. How does our single classifier option scenario pass? It seems like the classifier should never be used in such a case.

What is happening is that when we have only a single classifier option, the test data doesn't get changed from None. This means that the test input is None, and the `CopyCatClassifier` echoes it back for our test to pass. It's a complete accident. We should expose this by adding another test that ensures we'll hit this scenario. Here's the test:

```
def
given_a_different_single_classifier_option_that_does_not_require_
training_test():
    classifier_chooser =
ClassifierChooser.create_with_single_classifier_
option(AlwaysTrueClassifier())
    input_value = 42
    predicted_label = classifier_chooser.classify(input_value)
    assert predicted_label, "Should always predict True."
```

This gives an error saying that our class has no attribute `_classifier_options` which makes sense because we never set it if we don't find a perfect match. We should default to the first classifier in such a case. The following code gets our tests to pass:

```
def __init__(self,
             classifier_options_list,
             test_label=None,
             test_input=None):
    self._classifier_options = classifier_options_list[0]
    for classifier in classifier_options_list:
```

```
        predicted_label = classifier.classify(test_input)
        if predicted_label == test_label:
            self._classifier_options = classifier
```

Okay, our next test needs to get us using multiple inputs and labels to test accuracy. Here is a test that can drive us forward:

```
def
given_multiple_classifier_options_and_several_test_data_test():
    classifier_chooser = ClassifierChooser(classifier_options_list=[
            AlwaysFalseClassifier(),
            AlwaysTrueClassifier()
        ],
        test_input=[78,22,12],
        test_label=[1,1,0])
    predicted_label = classifier_chooser.classify(0)
    assert predicted_label == 1, "Should choose best classifier option
to classify with."
```

Surprisingly, the test passes if we put the `AlwaysTrueClassifier` first. This is because none of the predicted values would be a list, so the `ClassifierChooser` just opts for the first option by default. Setting the test up just as we have prevents this from happening. So now, we have a failure. We need `ClassifierChooser` to use our best performing classifier.

Here's an approach for getting the tests to pass again:

```
class ClassifierChooser:
    def __init__(self,
                 classifier_options_list,
                 test_label=None,
                 test_input=None):
        if not isinstance(test_label, collections.Iterable):
            test_label = [test_label]
            test_input = [test_input]
        self._classifier_options = classifier_options_list[0]
        highest_score = 0
        for classifier in classifier_options_list:
            number_right = 0
            for input_value, correct_value in zip(test_input,
test_label):
                predicted_label = classifier.classify(input_value)
                if predicted_label == correct_value:
                    number_right += 1
            if number_right > highest_score:
                self._classifier_options = classifier
```

We check the instance type as a temporary fix so that we don't have to refactor all of our tests, while also getting this test to pass. The reason we want to avoid this is that it very quickly leads us to a situation where we can lose control of our code.

Now that the tests are passing, we should refactor this hack out of our code. The first step is to change the test that uses a single training input and label to pass them in as lists of single items like the following:

```
def given_multiple_classifier_options_test():
    classifier_chooser = ClassifierChooser(classifier_options_list=[
            AlwaysTrueClassifier(),
            AlwaysFalseClassifier()
        ],
        test_input=[78],
        test_label=[1])
    predicted_label = classifier_chooser.classify(0)
    assert predicted_label == 1, "Should choose best classifier
option to classify with."
```

All the tests still pass. The next step is to remove the handling for all those that are being passed in as non-lists. When we make this change, many tests blow up. When we look through the code, it looks like it's taking place because we pass the label and input as none... Or more precisely, when we don't pass them in at all.

To fix this issue, we just need to change the constructor defaults like the following:

```
def __init__(self,
             classifier_options_list,
             test_label=[],
             test_input=[]):
```

All tests pass again!

Now, we need to add before the test the concept of training our classifier on the data. I'm going to cheat in a less-than-great way, and write the next test-oriented classifier without walking through the tests. At this point, you should be able to imagine how testing for the class would go. The following is the code for the tests and the class:

```
def given_a_dictionary_classifier_test():
    classifier = DictionaryClassifier()
    classifier.batch_train([
        (42, (1,2,3)),
        (2, (2,3,4)),
    ])
```

```
    assert classifier.classify((1,2,3)) == 42
    assert classifier.classify((2,3,4)) == 2

class DictionaryClassifier:
    def __init__(self):
        self._memory = {}
    def batch_train(self, observations):
        for label, observation in observations:
            if not observation in self._memory:
                self._memory[observation] = label
    def classify(self, observation):
        return self._memory[observation]
```

We can write a pretty simple test case (though more complex than our other test cases) to introduce training into our ClassifierChooser:

```
def given_multiple_classifier_options_and_several_test_data_with_
training_test():
    classifier_chooser = ClassifierChooser(classifier_options_list=[
            DictionaryClassifier(),
            AlwaysFalseClassifier(),
            AlwaysTrueClassifier()
        ],
        test_input=[(1,2), (3,4)],
        test_label=[3,7],
        training_inputs=[(1, 2), (3, 4), (5, 6)],
        training_labels=[3, 7, 11])
    predicted_label = classifier_chooser.classify((5,6))
    assert predicted_label == 11, "Should choose best classifier
option to classify with."
```

This test fails, so let's make it pass. When we introduce the concept of calling batch_train on the classifiers, we run into errors, because we haven't added this method to our simple test classifiers. We currently have a failing test as a result of this, so let's just add a do nothing batch_train method to each of our classifiers.

This is the updated constructor for our ClassifierChooser that gets our tests to pass:

```
def __init__(self,
            classifier_options_list,
            test_label=[],
            test_input=[],
            training_labels=[],
            training_inputs=[]):
```

```
        self._classifier_options = classifier_options_list[0]
        highest_score = 0
        for classifier in classifier_options_list:
            classifier.batch_train(zip(training_labels,
training_inputs))
            number_right = 0
            for input_value, correct_value in zip(test_input,
test_label):
                predicted_label = classifier.classify(input_value)
                if predicted_label == correct_value:
                    number_right += 1
            if number_right > highest_score:
                self._classifier_options = classifier
```

And this is what the updated simple classifiers look like:

```
class AlwaysTrueClassifier:
    def batch_train(self, observations):
        pass
    def classify(self, input):
        return 1
```

Only one of them is shown but, hopefully, this is enough to understand what happened. At this point, it seems like we're in a good-enough position to move onto using the `ClassifierChooser` with the Naïve Bayes and Random Forest classifiers, which we developed in the previous chapters, and then work on exploring the other options in scikit-learn.

Getting choosey

Next, let's explore hooking up the classifiers that we developed previously. We'll do it within our test framework, but we won't make it a true test yet. Let's just hook it up and poke at it with a stick to start off.

To do so, we can construct a test that must fail so that we can see the output of the strategically placed print statements within our test and `ClassifierChooser`. This test will be more complex, since it will more closely mimic a real-world scenario. Here it is:

```
def given_real_classifiers_and_random_data_test():
    class_a_variable_a = numpy.random.normal(loc=51, scale=5,
size=1000)
    class_a_variable_b = numpy.random.normal(loc=5, scale=1,
size=1000)
```

```
    class_a_input = zip(class_a_variable_a, class_a_variable_b)
    class_a_label = ['class a']*len(class_a_input)

    class_b_variable_a = numpy.random.normal(loc=60, scale=7,
size=1000)
    class_b_variable_b = numpy.random.normal(loc=8, scale=2,
size=1000)
    class_b_input = zip(class_b_variable_a, class_b_variable_b)
    class_b_label = ['class b']*len(class_b_input)

    classifier_chooser = ClassifierChooser(classifier_options_list=[
            CopyCatClassifier(),
            libs.NaiveBayes.Classifier(),
            libs.RandomForest.Classifier()
        ],
        test_input=class_a_input[50:500] + class_b_input[50:500],
        test_label=class_a_label[50:500] + class_b_label[50:500],
        training_inputs=class_a_input[:50] + class_b_input[:50],
        training_labels=class_a_label[:50] + class_b_label[:50])
    print classifier_chooser._classifier_options
    assert False
```

The libs.NaiveBayes.Classifier and libs.RandomForest.Classifier are
references to the code that we wrote in the previous chapters. In this test, you can see
that we just created a module for the classifiers to be in, so we can use them easily.
Starting at the top of this test, we create some kind of random data to represent some
sort of class that we call class a. After creating this data, we pull it together to match
the schema that our classifiers expect. Then, we do the same thing with the next
section, which is just us creating data to represent some imaginary class b.

Where we instantiate ClassifierChooser, we set our classifier options to be our
copy cat, Random Forest, and Naïve Bayes classifiers. Of course, we will expect our
CopyCatClassifier to do the worst. Based on the results of the previous chapter,
we will see the Naïve Bayes classifier outperform the Random Forest classifier.

Next, we pass in the training data. This data will be used to test how well the
classifiers have learned from the training data. We only take a small sample
of the full data to see how well the classifiers generalize.

Lastly, we print the classifier that our chooser ultimately chose. Inside the chooser, we've added a print statement to print out results of how well each classifier performed in our test. The constructor now looks like the following:

```python
def __init__(self,
             classifier_options_list,
             test_label=[],
             test_input=[],
             training_labels=[],
             training_inputs=[]):
    self._classifier_options = classifier_options_list[0]
    highest_score = 0
    for classifier in classifier_options_list:
        classifier.batch_train(zip(training_labels,
training_inputs))
        number_right = 0
        for input_value, correct_value in zip(test_input,
test_label):
            predicted_label = classifier.classify(input_value)
            if predicted_label == correct_value:
                number_right += 1
        if number_right > highest_score:
            self._classifier_options = classifier
        print('Classifier: {0}; Number right:
{1}'.format(classifier, number_right))
```

This is what your test output will look like:

```
-------------------- >> begin captured stdout << --------------------
Classifier: <choosey.CopyCatClassifier instance at 0x107433f38>; Number right: 0
Classifier: <libs.NaiveBayes.Classifier instance at 0x107433f80>; Number right: 811
Classifier: <libs.RandomForest.Classifier instance at 0x107433fc8>; Number right: 809
<libs.RandomForest.Classifier instance at 0x107433fc8>
```

As expected, our CopyCatClassifier was terrible and got nothing right. Your Naïve Bayes classifier may not have the batch_train method, so you may need to implement it. The Naïve Bayes classifier did better than Random Forest but just barely.

We developed the `ClassifierChooser` in isolation from the actual classifiers, because we wanted it to enable us to have a great amount of control in what the class does. We created some extra classes that are perhaps of limited value, but maybe not. By providing a set of simplistic sample classes, we enable other programmers to be able to drive our system with very simple test cases, as they try to learn more about it. On top of this, our test suite serves as a form of documentation that can show others how our code can be used. Using models that are somewhat silly require less assumed knowledge about specific machine learning algorithms. Just like our approach allowed us to develop one class at a time, it enables others to learn about one of our classes at a time.

Now, we can start digging in to scikit-learn to find new algorithms that we can snap into this admittedly simplistic platform.

Developing testable documentation

In this part of the chapter, we'll just explore different classifier algorithms, and learn the ins and outs of each.

Decision trees

Let's start with decision trees. scikit-learn has some great documentation, which you can find at `http://scikit-learn.org/stable/`. So, let's jump over there, and look up an example that states how to use their decision tree. The following is a test with the details greatly simplified to get to the simplest possible example:

```
from sklearn.tree import DecisionTreeRegressor

def decision_tree_can_predict_perfect_linear_relationship_test():
    decision_tree = DecisionTreeRegressor()
    decision_tree.fit([[1],[1.1],[2]], [[0],[0],[1]])
    predicted_value = decision_tree.predict([[-1],[5]])
    assert list(predicted_value) == [0,1]
```

A good place to start with the most classified algorithms is to assume that they can accurately classify data with linear relationships. This test passed. We can look for more interesting bits to test as well.

We can also write a larger test to show how effective decision trees are for the same kind of data that we've been classifying with Naïve Bayes and Random Forest classifiers. The test is built like the following:

```
def exploring_decision_trees_test():
    decision_tree = DecisionTreeRegressor()

    class_a_variable_a = numpy.random.normal(loc=51, scale=5,
size=1000)
    class_a_variable_b = numpy.random.normal(loc=5, scale=1,
size=1000)
    class_a_input = zip(class_a_variable_a, class_a_variable_b)
    class_a_label = [0]*len(class_a_input)

    class_b_variable_a = numpy.random.normal(loc=60, scale=7,
size=1000)
    class_b_variable_b = numpy.random.normal(loc=8, scale=2,
size=1000)
    class_b_input = zip(class_b_variable_a, class_b_variable_b)
    class_b_label = [1]*len(class_b_input)

    decision_tree.fit(class_a_input[:50] + class_b_input[:50],
                      class_a_label[:50] + class_b_label[:50])

    predicted_labels_for_class_a = decision_tree.predict(class_a_
input[50:1000])
    predicted_labels_for_class_b = decision_tree.predict(class_b_
input[50:1000])

    print("Class A correct: {0}; Class B correct: {1}".format(
            list(predicted_labels_for_class_a).count(0),
            list(predicted_labels_for_class_a).count(1)))

    assert False
```

We have the assert to make the test fail, so we can see the output that tells us how well the classifier did for each class. The output window will say something similar to when class a was predicted, it was right 835 times; when class b was predicted, it was right 115 times. It's a pretty lopsided classifier. Let's try upping the training size to see if it improves things.

The correct number actually fell, but only because we had fewer items in our test set, since we moved them to our training set. Mess with some other parameters and see if you can get the tree to perform better. In the meantime, we should add an assert along with a note of what we found.

This assert will do in our larger test:

```
assert list(predicted_labels_for_class_a).count(0) > list(predicted_
labels_for_class_a).count(1), "For some reason when
the decision tree guesses class a it's usually right way more than
when it guesses class b."
```

Let's create a quick class around our decision tree and throw it into our `ClassifierChooser` as well.

First, we need to put it into an adapter for the rest of our code to use it. This looks like the following:

```
import libs.DecisionTree


def decision_tree_can_predict_perfect_linear_relationship_test():
    decision_tree = libs.DecisionTree.Classifier()
    observations = decision_tree.batch_train(((44, (1,2)), ((10,
(45, 49)))))
    answer = decision_tree.classify((1,2))
    assert answer == 44, "Should be the answer it was trained on."
```

Now the test passes. Here is the adapter:

```
from sklearn.tree import DecisionTreeRegressor

class Classifier:
    def __init__(self):
      self._decision_tree = DecisionTreeRegressor()
      self._model = None
    def batch_train(self, observations):
        class_labels = map(lambda x: x[0], observations)
        class_inputs = map(lambda x: x[1], observations)
        observations = self._decision_tree.fit(class_inputs,
class_labels)
        pass
    def classify(self, observation):
        return self._decision_tree.predict(observation)
```

Another assumption that a decision tree has is that all of the data is quantitative and not qualitative (such as text or other similar things). As a direct result of this, we need to change our big test for the classes to be 0 and 1. On rerunning this bigger test, we'll see output similar to the following:

```
-------------------- >> begin captured stdout << --------------------
Classifier: <choosey.CopyCatClassifier instance at 0x10481b0e0>; Number right: 0
Classifier: <libs.NaiveBayes.Classifier instance at 0x10481b128>; Number right: 827
Classifier: <libs.RandomForest.Classifier instance at 0x10481b170>; Number right: 808
Classifier: <libs.DecisionTree.Classifier instance at 0x10481b1b8>; Number right: 780
<libs.DecisionTree.Classifier instance at 0x10481b1b8>

-------------------- >> end captured stdout << --------------------
```

Looks as though our decision tree did a fair bit worse than our other two algorithms. Also, we need to update our documentation test, and make it explicit that the decision trees need to be some kind of qualitative data.

This is how I tested this, and made it explicit in the beginnings of my documentation:

```
@nose.tools.raises(Exception)
def decision_tree_can_not_predict_strings_test():
    decision_tree = DecisionTreeRegressor()
    decision_tree.fit([[1],[1.1],[2]], [['class a'],['class
a'],['class b']])
    predicted_value = decision_tree.predict([[-1],[5]])
```

Summary

We covered a lot of material in this chapter. Once again, we covered moving incrementally in small steps in order to get specific software built. We also leveraged OOP to enable us to test our `ClassifierChooser` in isolation from our complex machine learning algorithms. Beyond this, we even leveraged creating extremely simple test classifiers to act as our way of decoupling from the more complex algorithms.

We now have the beginnings of a system that can test machine learning algorithms, and choose the best one according to some metric. We've also established a pattern to bring outside algorithms into our project, which includes wrapping the external library in an adapter. This ensures that you can bend the third-party library to your needs rather than bending your system around your third-party library, and making your code brittle (easily broken).

In the next chapter, we will be bringing all of the concepts that we've covered up to this point together. We'll have a project not unlike real-life marketing campaigns, where we will combine different machine learning techniques to maximize profit and minimize loss. We'll also dig deeper into leveraging scikit-learn while keeping it from tightly coupling to our code.

Bringing It All Together

In this chapter, we will consider what we've learned in previous chapters to solve a marketing problem. We'll be using some classification and regression techniques to optimize our spending on an ad campaign. On top of this, we'll build upon the previous chapter so that we can improve our models over time. Besides just using a simplistic measure of model quality, we'll dig in and automate some more metrics to control what we can push to production. The challenge that we'll be solving in this chapter will use something referred to as **uplift modeling**.

Here's the idea, let's say you want to launch a new mailing campaign to generate more business for yourself. Sending each letter costs a small amount of money so ideally, you'd like to only send this marketing campaign to the people who you have a reasonable chance of making money from (known as persuadables). On top of this, there are some people who will stop using your service if you contact them (known as sleeping dogs). In other words, the mailing may act as a sort of final straw for some people. On top of all of this, even if we only focus on people who we can persuade, some people will spend more money than others. Ultimately, we'd like to maximize our profit. How can we do this?

If we pick apart the problem description, a few things may pop out. To start with, we want to identify those people who we think we can persuade with the mailing. This sounds like a pretty solid exercise in classification. We don't know how we'll get our data yet, but we can discuss that in a bit.

The next thing you may notice is that we would like to optimize the profit that a specific person may yield, based on a set of data. This is a prediction problem, and not unlike classification. In this challenge, we'll probably try to maximize the expected value of each person that we send a mailer to.

To get this, we'll need a predictor of how likely each person is of being persuaded to buy from us. We'll also want another function that tells us if this person bought anything, and how much money do we expect him/her to spend? Since we're trying to maximize profit, we also need to take into account how likely this person is to stop being a customer because of this campaign, and how much money we stand to lose over the lifetime of the customer as a result. If we pull all of this together, we can describe our needs mathematically as the following:

- $P(B \mid C)$ = Probability of buying given the control (no ad campaign).
- *ExpectedProfit(C)* = Expected profit we will make from the customer assuming they decide to buy.
- $P(B \mid V)$ = Probability of buying given the variant (shown ad campaign).
- *AdCost(C)* = The cost to mail the ad to each specific customer. This is usually a constant like $0.40.

We can pull all of this together into a mathematical model like the following:

$$Profit(C) = P(B \mid V) * ExpectedProfit(C) - P(R \mid C) * ExpectedProfit(C) - AdCost(C)$$

Which simplifies to the following:

$$Profit(C) = ExpectedProfit(C) * [P(B \mid V) - P(B \mid C)] - AdCost(C)$$

This is definitely the most complex problem we've faced in the book, and this is once we *have* the data! Getting the data will also take some work. Let's work through each aspect of the model.

First, how can we build a predictive model for $P(B \mid C)$? Data around whether or not customers would purchase would be best generated as the result of a controlled test. We can identify some subpopulation of our customers and send the mailer to 50 percent of them, and the other 50 percent nothing. From this, we can tell how effective our mailer was at persuading people to change their behavior. If we assume that we have this data for each customer, along with variables to be used for prediction, then this seems pretty straightforward. Algorithm wise, we may be looking at Naïve Bayes, since we are looking for a standard probability. $P(B \mid V)$ seems like it should require the same approach.

For *ExpectedProfit(C)*, we basically have an input (our customer data). We want to predict an average amount that a customer like this might spend if he/she ordered it. This sounds like a regression problem.

AdCost(C) is best viewed as a constant. We won't worry about modeling this.

Starting at the highest level

There's a lot going on here. We can simplify it by just thinking about how to solve our high-level problem, and save the other solutions for later. Besides, we've already written the regression and classification algorithms. The worst case is that we may have to refactor them to work with the newer code that will use them. To begin with, we want to build a classifier that will identify the persuadables and sleeping dogs. Using this, we can optimize how we spend ad money to generate new business, and annoy as few of our customers as possible.

Here is one solid high-level test:

```
import nose.tools as nt

def given_a_sleeping_dog_test():
    classification_model = SimplisticClasses.
PersuadableAndSleepingDogClassifier()
    regression_model = SimplisticClasses.
AllCasesHaveSameProfitRegressionModel()
    customer = ('60602', 'male')
    ad_name = assign_ad_for(customer, classification_model,
regression_model)
    nt.assert_equal(ad_name, 'control', "Should let sleeping dogs
lie.")
```

Here, we have somewhat simplified the space by using a regression class that will just return the same results for every model. We can always add complexity later. The next thing we should pay attention to is that we don't have a PersuadableAndSleepingDogClassifier quite yet; we can build it though. In the following large test, we have a description of how this class should operate:

```
def
given_a_classifier_where_the_variant_improves_and_females_more_so_
test():
    classifier =
SimplisticClasses.VariantImprovesAndFemaleMoreSoClassifier()

    # Our persuadables
    order_probability = classifier.probability(('control',
'60626', 'female'))
    nt.assert_equal(order_probability, 0.60, "Females should have
a base probability of ordering.")
    order_probability = classifier.probability(('variant',
'60626', 'female'))
    nt.assert_equal(order_probability, 0.65, "Females should be
more likely to order with the new campaign")
```

```
    # Our no effects
    order_probability = classifier.probability(('control',
'60626', 'male'))
    nt.assert_equal(order_probability, 0.45, "Males should have a
base probability of ordering.")
    order_probability = classifier.probability(('variant',
'60626', 'male'))
    nt.assert_equal(order_probability, 0.45, "Males should be
equally likely to order with the new campaign")
    # More no effects
    order_probability = classifier.probability(('control',
'60602', 'female'))
    nt.assert_equal(order_probability, 0.70, "Females should have
a base probability of ordering.")
    order_probability = classifier.probability(('variant',
'60602', 'female'))
    nt.assert_equal(order_probability, 0.70, "Females should be
equally likely to order with the new campaign")

    # Our sleeping dogs
    order_probability = classifier.probability(('control',
'60602', 'male'))
    nt.assert_equal(order_probability, 0.50, "Males should have a
base probability of ordering.")
    order_probability = classifier.probability(('variant',
'60602', 'male'))
    nt.assert_equal(order_probability, 0.45, "Males should be more
likely to order with the new campaign")
```

This is a large test to write all at once in some ways. It has many assertions and has taken some thought. In our context, this is really about codifying how this should operate so that we have a single test case that exercises what we need. These specific probabilities were chosen so that we can have one segment of customers act as our persuadables, and have another segment act as our sleeping dogs. For the persuadables, you can see that the probability of ordering when exposed to our variant is expected to be higher (at the beginning of the test). The opposite happens with our sleeping dogs (at the end of the test). Also, I have a pretty strong intuition that the internals of this class are just going to be a static dictionary, where the probabilities can be looked up. Let's make the first assert in this set of tests to pass.

You can see this hunch taking shape by the time we get to the second test:

```
class VariantImprovesAndFemaleMoreSoClassifier():
    def probability(self, input):
        return {
```

```
        ('control', '60626', 'female'): 0.60,
        ('variant', '60626', 'female'): 0.65,
    } [input]
```

When the next test errors out, it says `KeyError: ('control', '60626', 'male')`.

This is not a great error, since it doesn't really tell us which test is failing. Let's add a new test that specifies if a given input is not contained in our class, then we return `None`:

```
def given_a_never_before_seen_observation_test():
    classifier = SimplisticClasses.
VariantImprovesAndFemaleMoreSoClassifier()
    probability = classifier.probability(('boo', 'bibbit'))
    nt.assert_equal(probability, None, "Should return None")
```

I will make this test pass with the following code:

```
class VariantImprovesAndFemaleMoreSoClassifier():
    def probability(self, input):
        data = {
            ('control', '60626', 'female'): 0.60,
            ('variant', '60626', 'female'): 0.65,
        }
        return data.get(input)
```

Once this test passes, we see a much better error message now —`AssertionError: Males should have a base probability of ordering.`

Perfect! Let's keep going. The rest of this will be pretty straight forward, so I won't walk through each test step by step. The finished class looks like the following:

```
class VariantImprovesAndFemaleMoreSoClassifier():
    def probability(self, input):
        data = {
            ('control', '60626', 'female'): 0.60,
            ('variant', '60626', 'female'): 0.65,
            ('control', '60626', 'male'): 0.45,
            ('variant', '60626', 'male'): 0.45,
            ('control', '60602', 'female'): 0.70,
            ('variant', '60602', 'female'): 0.70,
            ('control', '60602', 'male'): 0.50,
            ('variant', '60602', 'male'): 0.45,
        }
        if input in data:
            return data[input]
        else:
            return None
```

The next step is to build a simple regression class. As per the original test that we wrote, we want a class that embodies `AllCasesHaveSameProfitRegressionModel`. This should be an extremely simple implementation. Here's a test for it:

```
def given_any_input_test():
    regression_model =
SimplisticClasses.AllCasesHaveSameProfitRegressionModel()
    results = regression_model.predict(input=(42,'hai'))
    assert results == 12.25, "Should be a constant amount
regardless of the input."
```

And the tiny bit of code that makes this pass is given as follows:

```
class AllCasesHaveSameProfitRegressionModel():
    def predict(self, input):
        return 12.25
```

Now, if you rerun the tests, you will see that you're back to failing because of the original test. Specifically, `assign_ad_for` doesn't exist. Let's continue with the idea that our test classes are also production code, and let's define this function in the `SimpleTests.py` file. Our test moves on, and fails for a different reason now. We get the `AssertionError: Should let sleeping dogs lie` error.

Now, let's make this test pass. As a refresher, this is the test that we're working on to make pass:

```
def given_a_sleeping_dog_test():
    classification_model =
SimplisticClasses.VariantImprovesAndFemaleMoreSoClassifier()
    regression_model =
SimplisticClasses.AllCasesHaveSameProfitRegressionModel()
    customer = ('60602', 'male')
    ad_name = SimplisticClasses.assign_ad_for(customer,
classification_model, regression_model)
    nt.assert_equal(ad_name, 'control', "Should let sleeping dogs
lie.")
```

And this is the simple code that achieves this goal:

```
def assign_ad_for(customer, classification_model,
regression_model):
    return 'control'
```

Next, let's test that the system can recommend the ad that increases the probability to order it. This test is for such a case:

```
def
given_a_variant_that_improves_on_probability_of_ordering_over_control_
test():
    classification_model =
SimplisticClasses.VariantImprovesAndFemaleMoreSoClassifier()
    regression_model =
SimplisticClasses.AllCasesHaveSameProfitRegressionModel()
    customer = ('60626', 'female')
    ad_name = SimplisticClasses.assign_ad_for(customer,
classification_model, regression_model)
    nt.assert_equal(ad_name, 'variant', "Should choose to
advertise")
```

The following code gets this test to pass:

```
def assign_ad_for(customer, classification_model,
regression_model):
    control_probability_of_order =
classification_model.probability(('control',)+customer)
    variant_probability_of_order =
classification_model.probability(('variant',)+customer)
    return 'control' if control_probability_of_order >
variant_probability_of_order else 'variant'
```

Now, let's refactor a bit to make this more pythonic. My refactoring looks like the following (with passing tests checked along the way as I refactored):

```
def assign_ad_for(customer, classifier, regression_model):
    control_input = ('control',) + customer
    variant_input = ('variant',) + customer
    control_probability_of_order =
classifier.probability(control_input)
    variant_probability_of_order =
classifier.probability(variant_input)
    if control_probability_of_order >
variant_probability_of_order:
        return 'control'
    else:
        return 'variant'
```

Another thing that I notice about the design at this point is that `control` and `variant` essentially have the same sort of work done. Right now, this does not cause problems, and there's no test that should make this behave differently. Let's keep going and keep an eye on this.

Our next test is to test that, all things being equal, we should default to not advertise since that costs us money. Here's a test for this:

```
def
given_a_variant_that_does_NOT_improve_on_probability_of_ordering_over_
control_test():
    classification_model =
SimplisticClasses.VariantImprovesAndFemaleMoreSoClassifier()
    regression_model = SimplisticClasses.
AllCasesHaveSameProfitRegressionModel()
    customer = ('60626', 'male')
    ad_name = SimplisticClasses.assign_ad_for(customer,
classification_model, regression_model)
    nt.assert_equal(ad_name, 'control', "Should choose to NOT
advertise")
```

If you're like me, you might have thought that our code, so far, would already pass this. It doesn't though. Strangely enough, it looks like the way we coded this actually defaults to our variant, and we've caught a subtle bug! Of course, since we are using TDD, and we haven't written any tests around this behavior, it's actually just a feature that we haven't implemented yet. This might sound like a nit pick, but it's extremely important. It means that every line of the code which we create when we use TDD is explicit. It all exists to support some use case and there should be no extra code. Let's add this feature to our code:

```
def assign_ad_for(customer, classifier, regression_model):
    control_input = ('control',) + customer
    variant_input = ('variant',) + customer
    control_probability_of_order =
classifier.probability(control_input)
    variant_probability_of_order =
classifier.probability(variant_input)
    if control_probability_of_order >=
variant_probability_of_order:
        return 'control'
    else:
        return 'variant'
```

Just a simple greater than or equal sign saves the day. This leads us to our next test. Isn't there a set of tiny improvements that improves things, but not enough to make it worth the cost of advertising? Let's write a test to define such a scenario.

First let's plan out the scenario. We can see that females in the zip code `60626` see a probability to increase the order from 60 percent to 65 percent. With the profit amount that we've hardcoded, it gives each one a choice, and an expected value of $7.35 and $7.96 respectively. This means that if our ad cost were greater than or equal to this difference, we would not want to advertise to this customer. In this case, the difference is $0.61. Here's a test that encapsulates all of this:

```
def
given_variant_improves_over_control_but_not_enough_to_warrant_
advertising_cost_test():
    classification_model =
SimplisticClasses.VariantImprovesAndFemaleMoreSoClassifier()
    regression_model =
SimplisticClasses.AllCasesHaveSameProfitRegressionModel()
    customer = ('60626', 'female')
    ad_name = SimplisticClasses.assign_ad_for(customer,
classification_model, regression_model, ad_cost=0.61)
    nt.assert_equal(ad_name, 'control', "Should choose to NOT
advertise")
```

Here's the code that resolves the test failure:

```
def assign_ad_for(customer, classifier, regression_model,
ad_cost=0):
    control_input = ('control',) + customer
    variant_input = ('variant',) + customer
    control_probability_of_order =
classifier.probability(control_input)
    variant_probability_of_order =
classifier.probability(variant_input)
    lift = variant_probability_of_order -
control_probability_of_order
    expected_lift = lift * regression_model.predict(None) -
ad_cost
    expected_lift = int(100*expected_lift)/100.0
    if expected_lift <= 0:
        return 'control'
    else:
        return 'variant'
```

You can see that this requires adding or changing several lines. First, we define a default parameter that allows the other tests to operate without having to consider the ad cost (since we default it to $0.00). Next, we find the difference between the probability that the variant produces an order, and the probability that the control produces an order. Then, we can multiply this new percentage by the amount of money that we would make if this customer ordered, and subtract our small advertising cost. Lastly, we have to get this number to have only two decimal places. We make the choice to round down, since no one will ever round up the amount of money they give you.

When we predict the amount of money that the customer will give us, notice that we only pass in None. Once we start testing the regression side of this, it should change. For now, this is just something to keep an eye on.

Next, let's make sure that if we were to decrease our ad cost by just a hair, that the systems recommends advertising (since we're right on the edge of not advertising it in this test). The test will look like the following:

```
def
given_variant_improves_over_control_just_enough_to_warrant_
advertising_cost_test():
    classification_model =
SimplisticClasses.VariantImprovesAndFemaleMoreSoClassifier()
    regression_model =
SimplisticClasses.AllCasesHaveSameProfitRegressionModel()
    customer = ('60626', 'female')
    ad_name = SimplisticClasses.assign_ad_for(customer,
classification_model, regression_model, ad_cost=0.60)
    nt.assert_equal(ad_name, 'variant', "Should choose to
advertise")
```

It passes just as we expected. This seems like a great opportunity to move over and try different regression scenarios. Before we move on, there seems to be a good refactoring opportunity here. Notice that as we've been testing, we have only needed one bit of the state of VariantImprovesAndFemaleMoreSoClassifier at a time. We can probably make the tests more expressive (and much more readable!) by making this classifier use a dictionary that we can pass it in each test. It would also reduce the number of tests we need. This will be a great opportunity to show how we can extract a class out of this code without needing to write any new tests.

The first step that we should take is to introduce the class, and use it as a cheap stand in for our data dictionary. Notice that in this first step, our code takes a turn for the worse, but keep in mind that it's temporary:

```
class DumbClassifier():
    def __init__(self, state):
        self.state = state
    def probability(self, input):
        return self.state[input]


class VariantImprovesAndFemaleMoreSoClassifier():
    def probability(self, input):
        data = {
            ('control', '60626', 'female'): 0.60,
            ('variant', '60626', 'female'): 0.65,
            ('control', '60626', 'male'): 0.45,
            ('variant', '60626', 'male'): 0.45,
            ('control', '60602', 'female'): 0.70,
            ('variant', '60602', 'female'): 0.70,
            ('control', '60602', 'male'): 0.50,
            ('variant', '60602', 'male'): 0.45,
        }
        classifier = DumbClassifier(data)
        if input in data:
            return classifier.probability(input)
        else:
            return None
```

When refactoring code, each step of the effort is fixated on reducing risk. We want small isolated changes with a low likelihood of breaking something. In order to maintain our forward momentum, we should highly value making only those changes that we have a high degree of trust in. Rerunning our tests shows us that this didn't impact any behavior that we cared about. As we touched on before, "behavior we care about" is defined as behavior that we have explicitly written the tests for.

Next, let's get the if/else logic inside of our new object. Here's the next (tiny) step:

```
class DumbClassifier():
    def __init__(self, state):
        self.state = state
    def probability(self, input):
        data = self.state
        return data[input]
```

Here, we'll get the probability function to use variables with the same name so that we can easily transfer the if/then logic. Because of this change, it makes the next shift very copy/paste oriented:

```
class DumbClassifier():
    def __init__(self, state):
        self.state = state
    def probability(self, input):
        data = self.state
        if input in data:
            return data[input]
        else:
            return None


class VariantImprovesAndFemaleMoreSoClassifier():
    def probability(self, input):
        data = {
            ('control', '60626', 'female'): 0.60,
            ('variant', '60626', 'female'): 0.65,
            ('control', '60626', 'male'): 0.45,
            ('variant', '60626', 'male'): 0.45,
            ('control', '60602', 'female'): 0.70,
            ('variant', '60602', 'female'): 0.70,
            ('control', '60602', 'male'): 0.50,
            ('variant', '60602', 'male'): 0.45,
        }
        classifier = DumbClassifier(data)
        return classifier.probability(input)
```

Now, there's more that we could do to this class, but all of the logic has been shifted just as we wanted to, and we can start refactoring our tests to use our new class. Here's the first test that we can change as a result of this refactoring:

```
def
given_a_classifier_where_the_variant_improves_and_females_more_so_
test():
    classifier = SimplisticClasses.DumbClassifier({
        ('control', '60626', 'female'): 0.60,
        ('variant', '60626', 'female'): 0.65,
        ('control', '60626', 'male'): 0.45,
        ('variant', '60626', 'male'): 0.45,
        ('control', '60602', 'female'): 0.70,
        ('variant', '60602', 'female'): 0.70,
        ('control', '60602', 'male'): 0.50,
```

```
        ('variant', '60602', 'male'): 0.45,
    })


    # Our persuadables
    order_probability = classifier.probability(('control',
'60626', 'female'))
    nt.assert_equal(order_probability, 0.60, "Females should have
a base probability of ordering.")
    order_probability = classifier.probability(('variant',
'60626', 'female'))
    nt.assert_equal(order_probability, 0.65, "Females should be
more likely to order with the new campaign")


    # Our no effects
    order_probability = classifier.probability(('control',
'60626', 'male'))
    nt.assert_equal(order_probability, 0.45, "Males should have a
base probability of ordering.")
    order_probability = classifier.probability(('variant',
'60626', 'male'))
    nt.assert_equal(order_probability, 0.45, "Males should be
equally likely to order with the new campaign")
    # More no effects
    order_probability = classifier.probability(('control',
'60602', 'female'))
    nt.assert_equal(order_probability, 0.70, "Females should have
a base probability of ordering.")
    order_probability = classifier.probability(('variant',
'60602', 'female'))
    nt.assert_equal(order_probability, 0.70, "Females should be
equally likely to order with the new campaign")


    # Our sleeping dogs
    order_probability = classifier.probability(('control',
'60602', 'male'))
    nt.assert_equal(order_probability, 0.50, "Males should have a
base probability of ordering.")
    order_probability = classifier.probability(('variant',
'60602', 'male'))
    nt.assert_equal(order_probability, 0.45, "Males should be more
likely to order with the new campaign")
```

Of course, by keeping in mind what this new object does, we can verify that it works just as well by reducing this to a single case and assertion in this test. This reduced test now looks like the following:

```
def given_a_dumb_classifer_that_says_what_I_want_test():
    classifier = SimplisticClasses.DumbClassifier({
        ('control', '60626', 'female'): 0.60,
    })
    order_probability = classifier.probability(('control',
'60626', 'female'))
    nt.assert_equal(order_probability, 0.60, "Should return
probability I told it to.")
```

Then we have another scenario to test on this class. This happens when the input doesn't exist in the data that the DumbClassifier has provided. The test looks like the following after we overhaul it (the name remains the same):

```
def given_a_never_before_seen_observation_test():
    classifier = SimplisticClasses.DumbClassifier({})
    probability = classifier.probability(('boo', 'bibbit'))
    nt.assert_equal(probability, None)
```

After rerunning our tests, we'll find that everything passes. We won't rework all of the tests in this book, but we can work through one together so that you understand what I'm thinking. Let's work with the sleeping dogs test. It looks like the following, before our changes:

```
def given_a_sleeping_dog_test():
    classification_model =
SimplisticClasses.VariantImprovesAndFemaleMoreSoClassifier()
    regression_model =
SimplisticClasses.AllCasesHaveSameProfitRegressionModel()
    customer = ('60602', 'male')
    ad_name = SimplisticClasses.assign_ad_for(customer,
classification_model, regression_model)
    nt.assert_equal(ad_name, 'control', "Should let sleeping dogs
lie.")
```

Now, let's refactor this to use the new class, and work the context into the test directly, instead of hiding it in another class, as it was before. It looks like the following after our refactoring:

```
def given_a_sleeping_dog_test():
    classification_model = SimplisticClasses.DumbClassifier({
        ('control', '60602', 'male'): 0.50,
        ('variant', '60602', 'male'): 0.45,
    })
```

```
    regression_model =
SimplisticClasses.AllCasesHaveSameProfitRegressionModel()
    customer = ('60602', 'male')
    ad_name = SimplisticClasses.assign_ad_for(customer,
classification_model, regression_model)
    nt.assert_equal(ad_name, 'control', "Should let sleeping dogs
lie.")
```

Rerunning the tests shows that everything still works. At first glance, it seems like this refactoring just added more noise to our test. We should consider noise to be any information that isn't salient to the core of what the test is attempting to solve. In this case, this information seems very salient, and helps one to understand the test better. If anything that would have the object with all of these cases compiled into one spot was noisier, the reader would have to guess what the classifier was actually doing. They would also have to remember all of the hardcoded values. If we were to run into any issues in the first place, we had to switch to a file outside of our test, but then we had to read over the data structure with all of our test cases to decide which ones we cared about and which ones we didn't.

Next, let's go through the rest of the tests and refactor them like the next one (using the appropriate data for each one).

Oh, and there's one more refactoring that we can do. Now that the test's state is all in one place, we can remove the code duplication. The data that describes our customer is defined in three separate spots. We can probably reduce this to just one. We can do so as follows:

```
def given_a_sleeping_dog_test():
    customer_segment = ('60602', 'male')
    classification_model = SimplisticClasses.DumbClassifier({
        ('control',) + customer_segment: 0.50,
        ('variant',) + customer_segment: 0.45,
    })
    regression_model = SimplisticClasses.
AllCasesHaveSameProfitRegressionModel()
    ad_name = SimplisticClasses.assign_ad_for(customer_segment,
classification_model, regression_model)
    nt.assert_equal(ad_name, 'control', "Should let sleeping dogs
lie.")
```

Not only did we reuse our original definition of the data, but we also renamed it to express better what is going on. Suddenly, the data that backs our classification model points to what is the important information that we're adding in each line of the test.

Now that we've refactored everything, we have one last thing to do—remove the unnecessary `VariantImprovesAndFemaleMoreSoClassifier` class. Rerun the tests one last time just to be sure. Everything passes and our code is clean! Let's start driving some more functionality. For the next test, let's focus on how we use our regression class:

```
def
given_probability_to_order_remains_constant_but_expected_profit_
increases_test():
    customer_segment = ('60626', 'female')
    classification_model = SimplisticClasses.DumbClassifier({
        ('control',) + customer_segment: 0.65,
        ('variant',) + customer_segment: 0.65,
    })
    regression_model = SimplisticClasses.DumbClassifier({
        ('control',) + customer_segment: 12.25,
        ('variant',) + customer_segment: 15.50,
    })
    ad_name = SimplisticClasses.assign_ad_for(customer_segment,
classification_model, regression_model)
    nt.assert_equal(ad_name, 'variant', "Should recommend using
ad")
```

While writing this test, you may have also noticed that we can just reuse the `DumbClassifier` if we add a new method to the class. We'll probably want to rename it as well. On rerunning the tests, you'll see that the latest test is failing because the class doesn't have the `predict` function. So let's add it as follows:

```
class DumbClassifier():
    def __init__(self, state):
        self.state = state
    def probability(self, input):
        data = self.state
        return data.get(input)
    def predict(self, input):
        return self.probability(input)
```

There is some refactoring to do, but we need to get this test to pass first. Rerunning our tests gives us the following error:

```
TypeError: unsupported operand type(s) for *: 'float' and
'NoneType'
```

Remember how we just passed None into our regression class, and made a mental note that we should be forced to fix that at some point? This is that some point. Our previous code needs a little reworking to support this test case.

Before you just assume, let me tell you that the regression model will always return the same value (because it was). Now we need to find the expected value of both control and our variant to decide between them. The finished code fell together pretty fast, as I just broke down the line that handled the calculation into variable assignments. Here, this is after the tests pass, but before the refactoring:

```
def assign_ad_for(customer, classifier, regression_model,
ad_cost=0):
    control_input = ('control',) + customer
    variant_input = ('variant',) + customer
    control_probability_of_order =
classifier.probability(control_input)
    variant_probability_of_order =
classifier.probability(variant_input)
    control_profit = regression_model.predict(control_input)
    variant_profit = regression_model.predict(variant_input)
    expected_lift = variant_probability_of_order * variant_profit
- control_probability_of_order * control_profit   - ad_cost
    expected_lift = int(100*expected_lift)/100.0
    if expected_lift <= 0:
        return 'control'
    else:
        return 'variant'
```

The line got a bit long. Let's refactor a bit to decompose the line that does the main expected value calculation:

```
def assign_ad_for(customer, classifier, regression_model,
ad_cost=0):
    control_input = ('control',) + customer
    variant_input = ('variant',) + customer
    control_probability_of_order =
classifier.probability(control_input)
    variant_probability_of_order =
classifier.probability(variant_input)
    control_profit = regression_model.predict(control_input)
    variant_profit = regression_model.predict(variant_input)
    variant_expected_value = variant_probability_of_order *
variant_profit - ad_cost
    control_expected_value = control_probability_of_order *
control_profit
```

```
    expected_lift =  variant_expected_value -
control_expected_value
    expected_lift = int(100*expected_lift)/100.0
    if expected_lift <= 0:
        return 'control'
    else:
        return 'variant'
```

This makes it pretty easy to read, but notice that we can simplify this even further. Now that we've grouped the advertising cost into the expected value of the variant, we can just do a simple comparison and not even worry about the rounding numbers. Compare the previous refactoring to this one:

```
def assign_ad_for(customer, classifier, regression_model,
ad_cost=0):
    control_input = ('control',) + customer
    variant_input = ('variant',) + customer
    control_probability_of_order =
classifier.probability(control_input)
    variant_probability_of_order =
classifier.probability(variant_input)
    control_profit = regression_model.predict(control_input)
    variant_profit = regression_model.predict(variant_input)
    variant_expected_value = variant_probability_of_order *
variant_profit - ad_cost
    control_expected_value = control_probability_of_order *
control_profit
    if control_expected_value >= variant_expected_value:
        return 'control'
    else:
        return 'variant'
```

It seems like this should work, but it doesn't. This is due to the decision that we made earlier to round. Now it's codified in our tests. Realizing that this is what the problem boils down to, I regret the decision. Let's fix this. First, we should revert to our code that passes all of the tests. Next, let's change the test named given_variant_improves_over_control_but_not_enough_to_warrant_advertising_cost_test to the following:

```
def
given_variant_improves_over_control_but_not_enough_to_warrant_
advertising_cost_test():
    customer_segment = ('60626', 'female')
    classification_model = SimplisticClasses.DumbClassifier({
        ('control',) + customer_segment: 0.60,
        ('variant',) + customer_segment: 0.65,
```

```
    })
    regression_model =
SimplisticClasses.AllCasesHaveSameProfitRegressionModel()
    ad_name = SimplisticClasses.assign_ad_for(customer_segment,
classification_model, regression_model, ad_cost=0.6126)
    nt.assert_equal(ad_name, 'control', "Should choose to NOT
advertise")
```

We've changed the ad_cost from $0.60 to $0.6126. Now, we can refactor the code to state the fact that we're testing for a positive lift in our metric explicit:

```
def assign_ad_for(customer, classifier, regression_model,
ad_cost=0):
    control_input = ('control',) + customer
    variant_input = ('variant',) + customer
    control_probability_of_order =
classifier.probability(control_input)
    variant_probability_of_order =
classifier.probability(variant_input)
    control_profit = regression_model.predict(control_input)
    variant_profit = regression_model.predict(variant_input)
    variant_expected_value = variant_probability_of_order *
variant_profit - ad_cost
    control_expected_value = control_probability_of_order *
control_profit
    expected_lift =  variant_expected_value -
control_expected_value
    if expected_lift <= 0:
        return 'control'
    else:
        return 'variant'
```

Next, we can try out the kind of refactoring where we just compare the expected values. Changing our code to this causes our tests to still pass:

```
def assign_ad_for(customer, classifier, regression_model,
ad_cost=0):
    control_input = ('control',) + customer
    variant_input = ('variant',) + customer
    control_probability_of_order =
classifier.probability(control_input)
    variant_probability_of_order =
classifier.probability(variant_input)
    control_profit = regression_model.predict(control_input)
    variant_profit = regression_model.predict(variant_input)
    variant_expected_value = variant_probability_of_order *
variant_profit - ad_cost
```

```
        control_expected_value = control_probability_of_order *
    control_profit
        if control_expected_value >= variant_expected_value:
            return 'control'
        else:
            return 'variant'
```

Having gotten to this point, we're ready to move onto real algorithms and messy data.

The real world

Now that we have this harness built that can make recommendations on the customers that we should advertise to, we need to think about the kind of algorithms that we want to plug in it. For the probability of a customer placing an order, we can use Logistic Regression or Naïve Bayes. To estimate how much money the customer might spend, we can use (depending on our data) Gaussian Naïve Bayes or Linear Regression.

To start off with, let's use Linear Regression and Logistic Regression. The main purpose of doing this is to use more **sklearn** as, if we do, we won't have to spend time building the algorithms ourselves.

When we begin, it may be helpful to create a test file just to explore sklearn like in the previous chapter. We already have some generated data at `https://github.com/jcbozonier/Machine-Learning-Test-by-Test/blob/master/Chapter%209/fake_data.json`.

The Logistic Regression model in sklearn is only helpful if we can use it to get at the probability that someone will order. We should examine carefully whether it will work the way we want, before moving too far along with it. To this end, we can explore it first. Here is some code I wrote to explore this use case in a test:

```
treatment_codes = {
    'control': 1,
    'variant': 2
}
zipcode_codes = {
    '60626': 1,
    '60602': 2,
    '98006': 3
}
gender_codes = {
    'M': 1,
    'F': 2,
```

```
        'U': 3
    }
    def create_order_inputs_and_outputs(fake_data):
        test_inputs = []
        for x in fake_data:
            input = (treatment_codes[x['treatment']],
                zipcode_codes[x['zipcode']],
                gender_codes[x['gender']],
                x['orders_in_last_6_months'],
                x['customer_service_contacts'])
            test_inputs.append(input)
        test_labels = [x['ordered'] for x in fake_data]
        return test_labels, test_inputs


    def logistic_regression_hello_world_test():
        fake_data = json.load(open('./fake_data.json', 'r'))
        test_order_labels, test_order_inputs = create_order_inputs_and_
    outputs(fake_data)
        model = LogisticRegression()
        fitted_model = model.fit(test_order_inputs, test_order_labels)
        print(fitted_model)
        print(model.score(test_order_inputs, test_order_labels))
        print(model.predict_proba(test_order_inputs))
        assert False
```

Here, I've forced the test to fail so that the `print` statements will show me the output of the model. The sklearn API documentation is available at http://scikit-learn. org/stable/modules/generated/sklearn.linear_model.LogisticRegression. html.

To get this test to pass, we first have to encode all of the string values (gender, zipcode, and more from the previous data) as numbers, just as we would in Linear Regression. A handy way of doing this is to create dictionaries as we did previously. Once we have these, we can load the data from the disk, and create the input data in the kind of form that sklearn wants it in—one row at a time as a nameless list of positional data. The variables should be entered into the list in a consistent position.

Then, sklearn likes to have the classifications in a separate list, where the label situated at position *i* is the label for the input at the very same position. Then, we can just print out any information we're curious to see, and throw an `assert False` after we're done so that the test framework shows us everything that we've been writing to the console.

The `predict_proba` function seems to do what we're looking for. It returns a list that gives the probability of not ordering as the first item and the probability of ordering as the second item.

Let's create a simple class to wrap the Logistic Regression algorithm from sklearn. Our first test will look something like the following:

```
class DummySklearnModel():
    def __init__(self):
        self.predict_proba_call_arguments = None
    def predict_proba(self, input):
        self.predict_proba_call_arguments = input

def logistic_regression_test():
    dummy_sklearn_model = DummySklearnModel()
    model = SimplisticClasses.LogisticModel(dummy_sklearn_model)
    model.predict([1,2,3])
    nt.assert_equal(dummy_sklearn_model.predict_proba_call_arguments,
[1,2,3])
```

This dummy class exists entirely to act as a test construct. It basically pretends to be the `LogisticRegression` class from sklearn and collects the details, which lets us know that our `LogisticModel` class is performing its job correctly. We can get this test to pass with the following code:

```
class LogisticModel():
    def __init__(self, model):
        self.model = model
    def predict(self, input):
        self.model.predict_proba(input)
```

Next, we need to make sure that our adapter class returns the results of the `predict_prob` function call just as the rest of our code expects. To handle the case where we check to see what our `LogisticModel` class returned, we can do the following:

```
class DummySklearnModel():
    def __init__(self, probability_of_ordering):
        self.predict_proba_call_arguments = None
        self.probability_of_ordering = 0.42
    def predict_proba(self, input):
        self.predict_proba_call_arguments = input
        return [[1-self.probability_of_ordering,
self.probability_of_ordering]]

def logistic_regression_test():
    dummy_sklearn_model =
```

```
DummySklearnModel(probability_of_ordering = 0.42)
    model = SimplisticClasses.LogisticModel(dummy_sklearn_model)
    probability_of_ordering = model. probability ([1,2,3])
    nt.assert_equal(dummy_sklearn_model.predict_proba_call_arguments,
[1,2,3])
        nt.assert_equal(probability_of_ordering, 0.42)
```

Then, we just update our class like the following:

```
class LogisticModel():
    def __init__(self, model):
        self.model = model
    def probability (self, input):
        return self.model.predict_proba(input)[0][1]
```

Now, we are juggling between multiple models, and it can very quickly become confusing. We want our Logistic Regression classification model to work hand in hand with our Linear Regression model so that we can predict an expected value on a customer by customer basis. We're about to bring all of this together. Here is the first test for the regression model:

```
class DummyRegressionModel():
    def __init__(self, value_predicted):
        self.value_predicted = value_predicted
    def predict(self, input):
        return [self.value_predicted]

def linear_regression_test():
    dummy_regression_model =
DummyRegressionModel(value_predicted=33.12)
    model = SimplisticClasses.RegressionModel(dummy_regression_model)
    expected_profit_if_orders = model.predict([1,5,2])
    assert expected_profit_if_orders == 33.12
```

Notice that in these tests, I'm not actually testing sklearn. I'm essentially writing my tests, assuming that sklearn will do its job. I try not to test both the responsibilities of my code and these of sklearn simultaneously because it simplifies what I need to look at. Also, we should be able to trust that as long as we follow the contract implicit in their API, our code will work. We just want to be sure that we're wiring these different pieces together correctly. Here is the code that passes this test:

```
class RegressionModel():
    def __init__(self, model):
        self.model = model
    def predict(self, input):
        return self.model.predict(input)[0]
```

It is simple, but it will make sure that the models created by us will snap into place.

Now, this seems as though we have all of the pieces we need to assemble this system. We need to figure out how we'll test the output of the system at large. Let's write a bigger test to manage this for us.

This test will read our data from the disk, fit a model inside, and then tell us how much money the model could have saved over our control and variant.

Next, we set up the big, (almost) final stage of this exercise:

```
def the_big_test():
    fake_data = json.load(open('./fake_data.json', 'r'))
    test_order_labels, test_order_inputs =
create_order_inputs_and_outputs(fake_data)
    test_profit_labels, test_profit_inputs =
create_profit_inputs_and_outputs(fake_data)

    order_model = LogisticRegression()
    fitted_order_model = order_model.fit(test_order_inputs,
test_order_labels)

    profit_model = statsmodels.api.OLS(test_profit_labels,
test_profit_inputs)
    fitted_profit_model = profit_model.fit()

    profit_model =
SimplisticClasses.RegressionModel(fitted_profit_model)
    order_model =
SimplisticClasses.LogisticModel(fitted_order_model)

    for order_input in test_order_inputs:
        treatment_to_use =
SimplisticClasses.assign_ad_for(order_input[1:],
                                               order_
model,
                                               profit_
model,
                                               ad_
cost=0.50,
                                               variant_
map=treatment_codes)
        print treatment_to_use, order_input
    assert False
```

The one thing you may have noticed is that we need to be able to translate the treatment names and other data into the encoded values. By adding the expectation, I can map labels to numbers in this test, and we'll get most of what we need:

```
def given_classifications_that_are_numerical_test():
    customer_segment = ('60626', 'female')
    classification_model = SimplisticClasses.DumbClassifier({
        (1,) + customer_segment: 0.60,
        (2,) + customer_segment: 0.65,
    })
    regression_model =
SimplisticClasses.AllCasesHaveSameProfitRegressionModel()
    ad_name = SimplisticClasses.assign_ad_for(customer_segment,
                                              classification_model,
regression_model,
                                                ad_cost=0.6126,
                                                variant_map=
{'control': 1, 'variant':2})['chosen']
        nt.assert_equal(ad_name, 1, "Should choose to NOT advertise")
```

Next, let's push this test forward by seeing how the models perform versus having all customers get either **control** or **variant**. In order to report on this, I need to refactor my tests so that I can get back more data to report on. This is the reason why `['chosen']` is tacked onto the end of the `assign_ad_for` function.

This is the final test that ensures that the machine learning algorithm can find an improvement over the control and variation by choosing the best options of the two strategies. This test provides an idea for the matter that could be written to test the following:

```
def the_big_test():
    fake_data = json.load(open('./fake_data.json', 'r'))
    test_order_labels, test_order_inputs =
create_order_inputs_and_outputs(fake_data)
    test_profit_labels, test_profit_inputs =
create_profit_inputs_and_outputs(fake_data)

    order_model = LogisticRegression()
    fitted_order_model = order_model.fit(test_order_inputs,
test_order_labels)

    profit_model = statsmodels.api.OLS(test_profit_labels,
test_profit_inputs)
    fitted_profit_model = profit_model.fit()
```

```
    profit_model =
SimplisticClasses.RegressionModel(fitted_profit_model)
    order_model =
SimplisticClasses.LogisticModel(fitted_order_model)

    treatments_to_use = []
    for order_input in test_order_inputs:
        treatment_to_use =
SimplisticClasses.assign_ad_for(order_input[1:],
                                                order_
model,
                                                profit_
model,
                                                ad_
cost=1.0,
                                                variant_
map=treatment_codes)
        treatments_to_use.append(treatment_to_use)

    chosen_ev_sum = sum([treatment['chosen_ev'] for treatment in
treatments_to_use])
    control_ev_sum = sum([treatment['control_ev'] for treatment in
treatments_to_use])
    variant_ev_sum = sum([treatment['variant_ev'] for treatment in
treatments_to_use])
    print chosen_ev_sum, control_ev_sum, variant_ev_sum
    assert chosen_ev_sum > control_ev_sum, "Optimized expected
value should be better than NO advertising."
    assert chosen_ev_sum > variant_ev_sum, "Optimized expected
value should be better than ALWAYS advertising."
```

The strategy that gives us the largest expected value is the optimal strategy. The amounts that come out of the algorithm, if you're interested to know, are $24,196 for the blending strategy, $23,879, and $22,023 for the third place price. This means our hybrid algorithm could be saving the owner of the old system hundreds if not thousands of dollars. Rerunning the previous test shows that everything is still running quite nicely. As always, there's more we can do, but let's start to wrap this up so that you can go off on your own.

What we've accomplished

We've gone from machine learning algorithms like linear regression to difficult to wield tools like random forests, to building our own Gaussian Naïve Bayes tool. We've built a custom platform that helps us identify the models that perform the best, and choose the best one when it spins and washes everything.

We've also taken a very pragmatic approach to TDD. There are better things that we could be doing, but these will improve over time. The most important tip to keep in mind is to ask yourself why your tests are getting in the way (when they do), and how you can make your tests run faster whenever they start to run too slow.

Summary

In this chapter, we modeled a somewhat complex set of data for us to optimize the money that was spent on the given ad campaign. In the beginning of this book, I foreshadowed that we would be discussing measuring machine learning via profit. This is a great example of it. By combining multiple techniques, we can create models suited to solving real-world problems. On top of this, we saw some more ways of working with sklearn that prevents the coupling of your code with sklearn tightly.

Moving on from here, you can expect to spend less time manually implementing machine learning algorithms, and spending more time learning to use sklearn's built-in models. We haven't even tapped sklearn's pipeline features, nor its wide array of tunable parameters for the many machine learning algorithms that it supports. In most of the classification models, sklearn supports providing you a probability of a given classification. As we saw in this chapter, this can be a powerful tool when combined with our machine learning techniques, such as regression. More intersections of techniques like these exist, especially in the areas of probability and economics. Learning more about even just the simpler math, as we did here with the expected values, can lead to an ability to construct a composite machine learning model from a set of models that you've become more familiar with.

Index

J

Jarque-Bera test 55

K

Kaggle competition
    reference link 106

L

Likelihood Ratio p-value 74
Linear Regression
    using 158-164
logistic data
    generating 68, 69
Logistic Regression
    using 158-164

M

machine learning
    applying, to test-driven development
        (TDD) 10
model
    cross-validating 64
    foundation, building 56-63
    test driving 72-76
model accuracy
    measuring 70, 71
model quality
    quantifying 54, 55
Monte Carlo methods 36
multi-armed bandit algorithm 35
multiple coefficient of determination 55

P

perceptron
    about 21
    testing 22-33

Q

Q-Q Plot 55

R

Random Forest
    upgrading to 111-115
randomized probability matching
        bandit algorithm 43-45
randomness
    dealing with 11-15
real world situations
    simulating 40-42
regression
    about 16
    assumptions 54
ROC curve
    reference link 17
RPMBandit
    about 50
    versus SimpleBandit 50, 51

S

SimpleBandit
    about 50
    versus RPMBandit 50, 51
simplistic bandit algorithm
    building 37-40
simulation
    testing with 36
sklearn
    about 158
    URL, for documentation 159
straight bootstrapping
    problem 48, 49

T

test
    about 6-8
    anatomy 8
testable documentation
    developing 134
test-driven development (TDD)
    about 1-3, 117, 118
    applying, to machine learning 10
    reference link 118
    requisites 2

About Packt Publishing

Packt, pronounced 'packed', published its first book, *Mastering phpMyAdmin for Effective MySQL Management*, in April 2004, and subsequently continued to specialize in publishing highly focused books on specific technologies and solutions.

Our books and publications share the experiences of your fellow IT professionals in adapting and customizing today's systems, applications, and frameworks. Our solution-based books give you the knowledge and power to customize the software and technologies you're using to get the job done. Packt books are more specific and less general than the IT books you have seen in the past. Our unique business model allows us to bring you more focused information, giving you more of what you need to know, and less of what you don't.

Packt is a modern yet unique publishing company that focuses on producing quality, cutting-edge books for communities of developers, administrators, and newbies alike. For more information, please visit our website at www.packtpub.com.

About Packt Open Source

In 2010, Packt launched two new brands, Packt Open Source and Packt Enterprise, in order to continue its focus on specialization. This book is part of the Packt Open Source brand, home to books published on software built around open source licenses, and offering information to anybody from advanced developers to budding web designers. The Open Source brand also runs Packt's Open Source Royalty Scheme, by which Packt gives a royalty to each open source project about whose software a book is sold.

Writing for Packt

We welcome all inquiries from people who are interested in authoring. Book proposals should be sent to author@packtpub.com. If your book idea is still at an early stage and you would like to discuss it first before writing a formal book proposal, then please contact us; one of our commissioning editors will get in touch with you.

We're not just looking for published authors; if you have strong technical skills but no writing experience, our experienced editors can help you develop a writing career, or simply get some additional reward for your expertise.

Mastering Machine Learning with scikit-learn

ISBN: 978-1-78398-836-5   Paperback: 238 pages

Apply effective learning algorithms to real-world problems using scikit-learn

1. Design and troubleshoot machine learning systems for common tasks including regression, classification, and clustering.

2. Acquaint yourself with popular machine learning algorithms, including decision trees, logistic regression, and support vector machines.

3. A practical example-based guide to help you gain expertise in implementing and evaluating machine learning systems using scikit-learn.

Test-Driven Development with Mockito

ISBN: 978-1-78328-329-3   Paperback: 172 pages

Learn how to apply Test-Driven Development and the Mockito framework in real life projects, using realistic, hands-on examples

1. Start writing clean, high quality code to apply Design Patterns and principles.

2. Add new features to your project by applying Test-first development- JUnit 4.0 and Mockito framework.

3. Make legacy code testable and clean up technical debts.

Please check **www.PacktPub.com** for information on our titles

Machine Learning with R Cookbook

ISBN: 978-1-78398-204-2   Paperback: 442 pages

Explore over 110 recipes to analyze data and build predictive models with the simple and easy-to-use R code

1. Apply R to simplify predictive modeling with short and simple code.

2. Use machine learning to solve problems ranging from small to big data.

3. Build a training and testing dataset from the churn dataset,applying different classification methods.

Building Machine Learning Systems with Python
Second Edition

ISBN: 978-1-78439-277-2   Paperback: 326 pages

Get more from your data through creating practical machine learning systems with Python

1. Build your own Python-based machine learning systems tailored to solve any problem.

2. Discover how Python offers a multiple context solution for create machine learning systems.

3. Practical scenarios using the key Python machine learning libraries to successfully implement in your projects.

Please check **www.PacktPub.com** for information on our titles